Christian and Sikh

*Multiple Religious Participation
and Practical Theology*

— JOHN BARNETT —

Sacristy Press
PO Box 612, Durham, DH1 9HT

www.sacristy.co.uk

First published in 2021 by Sacristy Press, Durham

Copyright © John Barnett 2021
The moral rights of the author have been asserted.

All rights reserved, no part of this publication may be reproduced or transmitted in any form or by any means, electronic, mechanical photocopying, documentary, film or in any other format without prior written permission of the publisher.

Scripture quotations, unless otherwise stated, are from the *New Revised Standard Version Bible: Anglicized Edition*, copyright © 1989, 1995 National Council of the Churches of Christ in the United States of America. Used by permission. All rights reserved worldwide.

Every reasonable effort has been made to trace the copyright holders of material reproduced in this book, but if any have been inadvertently overlooked the publisher would be glad to hear from them.

Sacristy Limited, registered in England & Wales, number 7565667

British Library Cataloguing-in-Publication Data
A catalogue record for the book is available from the British Library

ISBN 978-1-78959-145-3

Dedicated to my grandchildren, Reuben, Arthur, Esme, Theo and Charlie.

"Is it not strange, that an infant should be heir of the whole World, and see those mysteries which the books of the learned never unfold?"
Thomas Traherne, Centuries of
Meditations, Chapter 3, section 2

Contents

Foreword v
Acknowledgements vii
Introduction 1

Chapter 1. Why multiple religious participation matters 11
Chapter 2. Settling in 22
Chapter 3. Holding it together 39
Chapter 4. Challenges 51
Chapter 5. Community identities 65
Chapter 6. Becoming different 84
Chapter 7. What's in a name? 99
Chapter 8. Changing interfaith practice 108
Chapter 9. An imaginative interlude 124
Chapter 10. The friendliness of God 137
Chapter 11. Taking stock 150

Coda 152
Appendix: Under the bonnet 153
Bibliography 164
Glossary 169
Notes 175
Index 190

Foreword

Have you ever wondered what would happen if a white Christian practising parish minister with decades of church experience were habitually to walk out from the normal Sunday service which he leads and go to worship every Sunday morning in addition in a local Sikh gurdwara, complete with clerical collar? How would his congregation feel? Would his bishop and colleagues tell him to stop? Would he be welcomed at the gurdwara? How would he manage without knowing Punjabi? Could he really become part of a Sikh community in a meaningful sense, or would he stick out like a sore thumb? Would he need to wear or turban – or never to wear a turban? Would he be able or willing to pray there? And to whom or what might be pray? How would his participation there affect his work in his congregation—and the people of the gurdwara? Would he lose his Christian faith? Or become some kind of hybrid religious person? And what would his family and friends make of his double allegiance and some of the changes of mindset and habits that might result? Would they think the whole thing an idiosyncratic, quixotic quest, or might they, too, benefit from the experience? Would it all be a positive, creative experience? Or might it all end in misunderstanding, disappointment and tears? What could possibly go wrong?

It may never have occurred to most readers of this book to ask these questions. But now that they have been mentioned, I hope you are longing to read on and explore these and other issues arising from John Barnett's intriguing, enjoyable and fascinating reflective account of his critical, costly and exhilarating experiment in Multiple Religious Participation. I was lucky enough to accompany John as an academic supervisor on his journey outside his own familiar context as a Christian parish minister and inter-faith officer. He learned a lot from it, and so did I. And now you have the opportunity to do so, too, in a wonderfully lucid account of his journey into a different space, community and theology.

I am sure you will enjoy meeting John and others in the pages of this book, and you will certainly not be bored. You will learn a good deal about John as person and pastor and how his views of himself and his faith engagement and practice were affected while he was undertaking research in the GKN gurdwara in Wolverhampton. You will also learn a great deal about Sikhism and the state of interfaith relations and dialogue, as well as the practical problems of trying to enter a religious group and culture that is not very familiar—a practical experiment in encountering otherness which is much talked about but seldom risked. John wears his learning lightly; you will find that you become more knowledgeable and critical without having information and theories thrust at you. Beyond this, you will be able to see that research is not a matter of cold, objective and objectifying enquiry, but a personally involving and transforming quest for greater understanding that is full of problems, mistakes, wrong turnings and plain howlers. Through all of this, John's own quiet, critical, appreciative and winsome voice comes through as a reliable guide to a complex endeavour, understanding a completely different culture, organisation and complex of theological presuppositions and practices. John's preparedness to leave his own comfort zone in pursuit of understanding and truth is inspiring, as is his clear willingness to be changed by what he experiences. And (spoiler alert) he is indeed changed in what he thinks and believes, not only in relation to Sikhism, but also in relation to his own Christian faith, as he develops a close relationship with the founder of Sikhism, Guru Nanak. One of the highlights of the book for me is a set of very moving reflective meditations on the relations between Guru Nanak and Jesus. Here research manifests itself as devotion and practical respect as John explores the notion of amicism, friendliness, to understand the creatively porous relationship of religions.

There is much originality in the way that John undertook and reports on his quest, and much that is pleasurable in how he writes about it as a vision of exploration and discovery unfolds. It is an honour to commend Christian and Sikh to its readers. Now I must stand aside to let John open the door of the gurdwara so you can follow him in.

Stephen Pattison
Formerly of the University of Birmingham

Acknowledgements

There are a few people who have asked that the details of their assistance not be identified, and so I am listing most acknowledgements without further identification and in alphabetical order.

Those listed include interviewees, members of focus groups, readers of the drafts and others who have helped over specific aspects of the research: Parmjit Singh Bahia, Tracey Bailey, Tony Barlow, Tia Berry, Inderjit Bhogal, Maxim Bolt, Jaswinder Singh Chaggar, John Paul and Dalbir Chauhan, George Chryssides, Irene and Tony Cornforth, Victor Dosanjh, John Fox, Jenny Gage, Amar Galkhal, Ray Gaston, Laurence Hillel, Michael Jaggasar, Angela Jagger, Jagbir Jhutti-Johal, Laura Johnson, Satvinder Juss, Sheila Maggs, Markhan and Jennifer Mann, Richard Martin, Louise Morris, Dal Padda, John Parry, Michael Redman, Erik Resly, Harsimranjeet and Gagandeep Short, Mak Singh, Andrew Smith, Peter Stribblehill, Opinderjit Takhar, Carlton Turner, and Tom Wilson.

My thanks also go to the committees of my host religious communities, the Sikhs of *Guru Ka Niwas Gurdwara* in Wolverhampton and the Christians of Beacon Church, Pheasey for their permission to engage in the research and to write about it, and for their encouragement while doing so; and to local clerical colleagues and individuals in the Church and in the wider Sikh fellowship, the *sangat*, whose names I have not had agreement to make public and so who are not otherwise recognized. I have also greatly appreciated the wisdom and camaraderie of researching colleagues at Birmingham University over the years: Peter Babington, David Beedon, Sian Hancock, John Itumu, Nick Ladd, Mark Pryce, Asgar Rajput, Dawn Saunders, Megan Smith, Mark Stobert, Tim Welch, and Jo Whitehead, and the staff who have supported us: Mark Cartledge, Jeremy Kidwell, and Chris Shannahan. David Primrose's hospitality to researchers in Lichfield Diocese was a further blessing. It has been enjoyable to continue in this sense of a shared objective working with

Sacristy Books. My Commissioning Editor, Natalie Watson, gave her vital initial support for the book and has continued with a judicious mixture of encouragement and challenge, in which she has demonstrated her depth of engagement with practical theology and interreligious writing. Sarah Parkinson also brought careful attention to her role of copy-editor. I am grateful to them both.

Turning to those to have taken particularly significant parts in the research there are my Christian collocutors, Warren Bardsley, who set me on my way, and Deb Dyson, who picked up from him with enthusiasm. My Sikh collocutor, Bhajan Singh Devsi, not only filled that role but also acted as my advocate with the gurdwara committee and as my informant on all things Sikh, in weekly chats and regular longer sessions. Mark Stobert, my spiritual adviser, took on the role of reflection partner, helpfully clarifying some issues and—equally helpfully—confusing others.

And so to those at the apex of this platform of support and assistance, starting with Clive Gregory, the Bishop of Wolverhampton, who supported me throughout the length of this research despite the potential for controversy it represents, and arranged for significant funding from the Diocese of Lichfield, to which I also give thanks. My academic guide, Stephen Pattison, has throughout shown that blend of erudition, experience, rigour, and kindness for which he is well known across the community of practical theology, and I am very grateful to him. The most heartfelt thanks are reserved for Janice, my wife, who has supported me throughout this long endeavour. I have found many ways to test her patience over the years, but spending the first years of our retirement—including the warmest summer for decades—stuck up in the attic tapping away on the computer has been greeted only with encouragement and affectionate support.

As I thank people, so it should be made clear that errors and strange opinions should not be attributed to any of the many people who have helped me. In particular, I should say Bhajan is not responsible for any erroneous views I have expressed on *Sikhi*. There would have been many more without his treasured guidance.

Introduction

Setting out

A member of the congregation was recalling her childhood memory of hanging days at Birmingham prison, and—macabre or not—she had our attention: "A notice went up at eight in the morning to say someone was to be hanged, and another an hour later to say that they have been buried within the grounds. 'Up at eight, down at nine,' we would say." Such a striking reminiscence was a conversational challenge, and I could sense her listeners readying to take up the gauntlet with colourful stories of their own. I had always enjoyed this stage after a service when, over coffee, people had finished with the business of the day and moved on to the relaxed pleasure of just chatting, but now I was conscious of another engagement pulling me away. It was that time on a Sunday when I headed off from the folk I pastored and drove thirteen miles up the motorway to the Sikh gurdwara where I was also a regular worshipper. Less than two hours after preaching and presiding at Holy Communion I would be lying prostrate before the Sikh scriptures, *Guru Granth Sahib Ji*, and joining in, as best I could, the worship there. How and why I had begun this multiple religious participation (MRP), what it entailed, how it affected me, and why I am now sharing that experience more widely are the subjects of this book. Readers may well have their own views on the wisdom of this course of action. Whether initially critical or welcoming I invite you to read the whole story before coming to judgement. It is a story that is not only personal but also rooted in wider social changes, changes that invite a fresh exploration of the relationship of Christianity with other faiths.

In this Introduction, I acknowledge aspects of my own religious background that made me open to MRP, and I explain why I particularly sought to engage with Sikhs. Chapter 1 outlines the nature and importance of MRP in the wider cultural and religious setting and locates my own exploration in that context. Chapter 2 describes how things were when I started this engagement, how I was experiencing church life at the time, and how Sikh engagement began to affect me. There is an observer's view of the gurdwara, reflecting my initial place as an outsider. Chapter 3 describes being stuck in the role of welcome visitor, without any obvious development, being "held in orbit". I consider the effect of being in a Punjabi language environment, how my physical body linked two different experiences, and then explore how I was coping with the differences between Christian and Sikh beliefs. Chapter 4 draws together the challenges I faced: difficulties over getting permission to conduct the research in the first place, struggles over language, reactions from others, my own continuing anxiety over loyalty and betrayal, and issues arising from my family life. Chapter 5 considers religious identity as a matter for the community as well as the individual. It looks in detail at *Sikhi* as a faith identity, a nationality, and as an ethnicity, and how I related to that.[1] Parallel consideration is given to Christian identity, and to local belonging to the gurdwara and the church. I consider how my gender and sexuality affected my belonging to both faiths. Chapter 6 describes how the static role of "welcome visitor" at the gurdwara gradually changed as personal Sikh religious practice developed along with a commitment to Sikh *seva* (service). Continuing errors and corrections are acknowledged, but then I record the positive Sikh, interreligious and Christian responses to my work when my paid ministry and my formal research (but not my engagement) came to an end. Chapter 7 considers the issue of what I call myself, how that varied as the research went on, and how that depends on the circumstances in which I am talking. Chapter 8 relates my findings to the growing discussion in religious studies about the complexity of belonging, and addresses Christian interfaith workers and the wider Church, encouraging boldness in engaging more deeply with other religions. Chapter 9 uses imaginative work as a way of expressing the mutual friendship of Jesus and Guru Nanak and my own connection with it. Chapter 10 explores that friendship to make a link between my experiences and formal theology, suggesting divine friendliness, "amicism", as the key to interreligious relations. There is then in Chapter 11 a brief "taking stock", appropriate for a continuing story which has yet to reach its conclusion. An appendix follows, which explains some of the mechanics of what I was doing, and the techniques of autoethnography, practical theology and professional reflection that I was using. Some readers may prefer to turn to this more technical material after Chapter 1 in order to inform their reading of the rest of the book. Each chapter concludes with a handful of brief focal points. The story itself is the main thing, but these are intended to crystallize issues thrown up by the narrative.

My background

I have my own (changing) viewpoints, as with all writers, some of which can be explained by my personal history. My background has its place in the ongoing movements of migration that brought first Christianity and then *Sikhi* to these shores. Mother's family talked of Huguenot antecedents; Father's carried vague suggestions of Italy and Judaism. Both families were by the nineteenth century embedded in the masonic and Free Church life of Birmingham,[2] but my father became an Anglican churchwarden, and I was baptized and confirmed as an Anglican. I had three distinct Christian awakenings at school: a Scripture Union visitor came every week to lead a scrummage of bored, mischievous, and rather cruel little boys to the Lord, and I was struck by his respect and kindness towards us; there were weekly parades to Matins in the parish church, where I had a sense of a presence which seemed unnoticed by the busy and important people—clergy, choir, teachers—around me; then when I was fifteen we were given that radical Christian bombshell, John Robinson's *Honest to God* (1963),[3] to study, demolishing any tendency to regard Christianity as childish. The resulting strands have stayed with me: a connecting of true Christianity with respect and kindness; a sense of the numinous; intellectual curiosity; and an ambivalent attraction to and criticism of churchiness.

After ordination aged twenty-five, life carried on pell-mell as I got married, had two children, moved to larger parishes and took on various diocesan roles. Then I came to my fifties and a late midlife crisis, which took the traditional clerical form of a loss of faith, or rather loss of faith in the cumbersome superstructure of Christian doctrine. I retained a personal loyalty to Jesus alongside a continuing affection for the community of the Church and even the institution in its current weakened form, but had lost confidence in doctrinal formulations, seeing them as attempts by authorities, secular and ecclesiastical, to harness the power of religious experience for their own political ends. I mentioned it to my bishop at the time and he took what I was saying seriously, inviting me to come and discuss where I was heading. It was against this unsettled background that I was running on the treadmill in March 2007 at the local municipal gym:

> I started to pay attention to the pattern the sunlight was making from behind me, a silhouette of silver light round a black human shape. It seemed to be not just my silhouette, but a sign of the glory of all humankind. Then that was overlaid with the presence of Jesus, there with me. His glory was visible, the silver light had turned to gold, still radiating out of the human shadow in which it was hidden. He invited me to continue exploring the wounds in his hands, which I realized I had been doing for many months. I felt an overwhelming awe at the humility and generosity of Jesus in patiently allowing this. A feedback developed, in which the more I was aware of his humility the more I was aware of his glory, which in turn made me more aware of his humility and so on until I felt I would burst. I now know that no description of him can be glorious enough. I found myself repeating silently over and over "alleluia, alleluia!" in an attempt to let off steam.

I was intensely happy throughout the day, telling Janice, my wife, that something had happened, then describing it as best I could the next day. It left me with the conviction that belonging to the Church is a gift to be received in thankfulness, not the temptation to spiritual compromise I had feared. I realized Christ "does not need or seek to diminish the glory of others. In his light the glory of Muhammad or the Buddha shines more clearly than ever."[4] The day before I had argued with a man who had pinched my car parking space, as I saw it at the time. After this experience I had a longing to apologize and hung about the carpark trying to find him.[5]

Such religious experiences, like wasp stings, are noted for giving to those who undergo them a certainty that something has really happened to them, and I shared that. I tried to sort out how I knew that the figure I saw was Jesus and can only say that an integral part of the experience was that he revealed himself. Those who have tried to evaluate such events look for, along with certainty: a) immediate practical outcomes; b) healing; c) change of relationships; d) comfort; and e) good feelings; of which I experienced all except healing. For the Catholic Church, encouragement of established doctrines is a key test, against which my experience was ambivalent, although even by that standard I was probably in a better state afterwards than I was before in that I had reached a peace about doctrinal things which—if not quite acceptance—took away the urge to challenge. The vision felt liberating and permissive, opening the door to something new in my life. I was keen to see how this would unfold.

Meanwhile in my parish ministry I had been drawn, without any clear plan, into interreligious engagement. One of my churches hosted the local interfaith network to which I offered what support I could, and in another we employed a community worker and shared a building in partnership with a Muslim group and a Pentecostal church. I was interfaith workplace chaplain to our local council offices and was asked to chair a mayoral commission to examine the relationship between the council and different faith communities. As a result of my council role, a large Hindu temple invited me onto their community liaison committee, which was preparing for a visit from Rowan Williams, then Archbishop of Canterbury. It was at that visit that I first met Clive Gregory, the Bishop of Wolverhampton, who told me of his intention to appoint an interfaith officer to the area for which he had oversight. It was to be a half time post, with the other half in a parish.[6] I went home excited at the news, with a sense of things slotting into place. I applied and was appointed in October 2009.

The Church of England has a national interfaith programme known as *Presence and Engagement*, and every diocese in the Church of England is supposed to have a related post. They are identified collectively as Diocesan Inter Faith Advisers (DIFAs)[7] despite having a variety of individual job titles, and there is variety in the way different post-holders operate. I prioritized networking, so that I could connect Christians and members of other faiths who wanted to improve relationships, inform Bishop Clive of events and issues affecting other faiths in the area, and be in a position to draw people together when events required. This formation of friendships was demanding of time but was very enjoyable and felt worthwhile, despite such links being dismissed in a national report as "'saris, samosas and steel drums' for the already well-intentioned".[8] However, in July 2015, in the sedate setting of the County Hotel Walsall, I felt my easy-going approach coming under challenge. I had joined with people of different faiths to mark Srebrenica Day, reflecting on the massacre in 1995 of 8,000 Bosniaks by their Serb neighbours, and the descriptions of people who had been neighbours and friends participating in genocidal murder made the blood run cold:

> Prior to the war we all lived peacefully together. At school, [. . .] boys would grab a ball and play football, two teams against each other, not divided by religion. [. . .] Then came 1992. When the local government in Prijdor was overthrown by the Serbian 'Democratic' Party led by Karadžić, everything went downhill.[9]

I feared that the friendships in which I was engaged and which I was encouraging in others were merely masking identity traits which could at any time be summoned forth in anger or fear by the wicked or the thoughtless. It is plain to see this was no idle fear but has become a recurrent story across the world. Miroslav Volf, himself Croatian, wrote that human beings are as likely to hate their neighbours as to love them, since they are all too easily experienced as rivals to the same territory, and said that the only way to get to the root of this hostility was to be ready to rewrite our own identities. Over religion he called Christians to seek a deeper truth and not to cling to those facets of faith—those lies, he called them—that bolster our sense of self-importance or victimhood in the face of others.[10] Acknowledging that all my relationships begin from a Christian position I began to want to challenge my own identity to the point that "the other" was having some sort of effect on who I was, moving my boundaries. This Srebrenica Day challenge to allow myself to be reshaped worked together with the invitation from the vision to continue exploring the grace of Jesus, and I started recalling and looking for occasions in my interfaith work where the boundaries of religious identity might prove more porous than usual.

In 2013, a local imam had asked for my thoughts on a young man in his congregation who had come to him for advice. The young man had dreamed that while he was in the mosque the prophet Isa (whom Muslims identify with Jesus) had come to him, and that Isa had delivered a blessing for the whole community, standing as he did so by a window from which the local parish church was visible. When I went to the church to discuss it there, the vicar told me in turn of a vision someone had recently had of the waters of God's love flowing out into the wider neighbourhood. It seemed that although the young man was acting as a faithful Muslim, he and his imam were graciously engaged with something that might reasonably be considered Christian witness, especially if the vision in the nearby church was seen as confirmation. In subsequent discussions I found Christians and Muslims were divided between themselves as to the significance of the dream, some supportive, others dismissive, and I was myself puzzled enough to undertake a wider consideration of dream interpretation, but I remember most of all my awe that our (Muslim and Christian) God was at work.[11]

On another occasion in 2013, I had helped to arrange a gathering of distinguished Sikhs at a memorial marking the Anglo-Sikh Wars (1845–49) in Lichfield Cathedral. Sikh prayers were included in this peaceable event, and a number of Christians, including members of the cathedral chapter there as hosts, bowed their heads. Were they just showing their respect, or were they engaging in Christian prayers parallel with but separate from their guests? Or were they, as it felt to me in that atmosphere of reconciliation, in some way joining in?

The Hindu temple where I had met Bishop Clive had dedicated seven surrounding hillocks to different world religions in a gesture of interreligious solidarity.[12] The occasion for the Archbishop's visit had been his unveiling of a plaque with a scriptural text on the "Christianity" hill, and in 2015 a local Anglican priest was invited to conduct a service of Holy Communion there. The weather on the day drove the service into their community hall but as we worshipped, the identity of this worship,

Christian or Hindu, did not seem settled. The order of service and the leader were Christian, but the great majority of those present were Hindu. Although they were asked not to take communion the sternest observer could not deny that they were in some way participating, joining in this worship of Christ in a spirit of Hindu inclusiveness. Such thought-provoking experiences encouraged me in my attempt to deliberately cross religious boundaries and to do so in a reflective way, trying to recognize at every stage what was happening to me and any effect it might be having on the religious communities involved.

Such flexing of religious boundaries often arises through the lure of an attractive second religion, but mine was a less specific impetus so I needed to make a choice as to the religion with which to engage. I had sensed the attractions of many other religions in my role, though often aware (as with Christianity) of gaps between ideal presentations and the compromised realities of community and history. In the end, my choice was made on pragmatic grounds. I was to remain a Christian but chose *Sikhi* as the other religion with which to engage, partly because it is well represented in the area in which I worked; 9.1 per cent of the population of Wolverhampton, the second highest proportion in any local authority in Britain, make it an easy community to contact, and it is well established, not vulnerable in the face of any attention I may draw to it. *Sikhi* also represents an under-researched area of Christian interaction compared with Judaism, Islam, Hinduism or Buddhism, which was something I regretted. Further, I had experienced Sikh hospitality over the years and knew something of their theological openness and restraint over conversion, but also recognized a cultural and historical distinctiveness, a combination I hoped would make for a rich experience. Its links with the Vedic religions and through Islam with the Abrahamic tradition also added to the interest it offered. All that I had heard about Guru Nanak made me happy to explore a closer relationship with him and the religion he had established, so if there was no irresistible pull drawing me into *Sikhi* there was nonetheless a genuine appreciation and an excitement about what was to be learned.

In August 2015, before I began my research, I made a note of my then understanding of *Sikhi*, which I had first encountered in Smethwick in 2003. I knew something of Guru Nanak's (1469–1539) teaching against formulaic religion, encouraging meditation, good ethical behaviour, and discouraging ascetic practices that overwhelmed family and economic responsibility. He was also an advocate of equality of genders and disregard of caste, both of which were extraordinary for his time and place, and both of which have proved difficult for his followers to live up to. I was aware of the central place of the scriptures, *Guru Granth Sahib Ji*, and some of the practices used in worship. "Sikh" just meant "student", but I believed that *Sikhi* had taken on a more defined identity including the *Khalsa*, the community of initiated Sikhs, in the face of Muslim persecution (a view which was to be corrected). I knew that there were a few white, *gora*, Sikhs, especially in America, but that they tended to have unorthodox views and were regarded with suspicion by Punjabis. I was aware of some good relations between Sikhs and Hindus and that there were even some Hindu families with a tradition of one brother becoming a Sikh, but that Hindu-Sikh relationships had been badly damaged by the invasion of the Golden Temple in 1984 and the massacre of Sikhs after the murder of Indira Gandhi. I knew that attitudes towards Britain were mixed, with pride in the Sikh military role in the world wars standing alongside a contrasting pride in the Sikh part in freeing India from British rule; and pleasure at the achievements of the community in this country living alongside an awareness of racist attitudes here. I had, then, the background knowledge that engagement in interfaith work with Sikhs and a certain amount of general reading had brought, but it was an outsider's view, inevitably superficial.

Interreligious relations can operate at all sorts of levels: they can just be concerned with maintaining the peace; or with getting to know about other religions in a respectful but distant way. I was trying to move beyond that, to allowing the experience to change me, and I had to acknowledge there was a risk this would weaken my relationship with Jesus Christ. I was nonetheless willing to take that step based on the assurance of the vision, the urgency of the Srebrenica Day experience, and the knowledge that it could help my understanding of a major religious and cultural issue that was already shaping my professional life.

Focal points

1. This story is likely to come under judgement as it is read, and that is intended by the author, to invite the reader to reach a decision.
2. This is an idiosyncratic story revealing my own experiences and my (changing) viewpoint. However, that personal engagement is not a distortion of objective description and theory but a necessary window.
3. Interfaith work can and should reach a level where, for the parties engaged, it raises questions about their own identities.
4. There are already many situations in which the boundaries between religions become confused without this being acknowledged or investigated.

1

Why multiple religious participation matters

Awareness and engagement

My engagement in worship as a Sikh while continuing to worship as a Christian is an example of MRP, a pattern of participating in more than one religion. The recognition of this as a widespread if controversial activity and the desire to better understand it have led to an explosion of writing in which many terms are used, among them: "multiple religious belonging" (MRB) and "dual belonging", which point to religious commitment but perhaps without communal activity; "multiple religious practice", which again includes purely private devotion and belief; "back-and-forth riteing", where whole communities engage in rites of more than one religion; "hybrid" religion, which celebrates flexibility of identity but is an offensive term for some hearers, being a word found in the history of British racism;[13] and "syncretism", which carries a negative sense despite recent attempts at rehabilitation. "Hyphenated Christianity" is another term used, though I have not come across any other religion being so adorned. While recognizing the overlap between these various concepts I have stuck with calling what I am doing MRP, because my emphasis is on taking part in the religious lives of two faith communities and on achieving the fullest participation I can in the worship itself. Despite MRB being the phrase most widely used, I have preferred to say I was engaging in MRP because to what extent the participation would lead to belonging was uncertain; it was one of the main things I was trying to find out.

There are many different reasons for and ways of engaging in MRP. It may arise from the cultural setting, where religion is not so much a matter of belonging but of use, with religions like tools in a toolbox for different life events: "Shinto for the living, Buddhism for the dead."[14] Through Western eyes MRP is taking place, but this is not how those taking part see it, though even in this flexible setting most religious traditions expect their religious professionals to stick to one religion, a qualification important in my own case and that of my fellow DIFAs.

A person's MRP background may be due to their family structure rather than arising from the wider community. It is well known that mixed-faith families can face hostility, though I interviewed a number of people from mixed Sikh/Christian backgrounds who were positive about it, including married couples who maintained some level of joint practice without difficulty. Susan Katz Miller has written about her Jewish/Christian family, acknowledging some difficulties but being positive overall about her mixed-faith experience.[15] Children of dual-religion families are described as finding that duality to be a positive background and have an integrity of their own, so that if people are perplexed or offended by their saying that they have two religions and ask them to explain themselves, they reply "I just am." One correspondent told me of a colleague who had shared

> ... how much she admired her parents for bridging a seemingly unsurmountable divide by marrying across Hindu–Muslim religious lines, and how their resilience, their faith, their devotion to love, inspired and empowered her as a woman of colour in the United States. She has in them a model of what divine love looks like in practice.

MRP can arise as an aspect of the missionary desire to interpret Christianity into a culture where it is not familiar. Heroes of Christian interreligious activity such as Vincent Donovan, Jules Monchanin, Swami Abhishiktananda, and Bede Griffiths have sought to enculturate Christianity by entering a culture new to them; others have sought to exercise their Christian faith while continuing in the other-faith culture of their birth, such as Michael Rodrigo and Aloysius Pieris. As culture usually has religious aspects, this engagement is likely to have consequences for both the host culture and the introduced religion, as well as producing real tension in the quest for some sort of fusion without loss of integrity.

Some individual Christians engage with other faiths as a form of borrowing intended to enhance their own understanding and practice of Christianity. In the West, many draw on Buddhism, something which may not involve engagement with living Buddhist communities, but be an intensely personal and individual practice. "Passing over" takes this one step further, seeking to relativize both religions, opening a window to a mystery beyond, a process in which Christian identity can be lost. The approach of the borrower is essentially unequal, with the religion visited having a secondary role, and it can give rise to resentment, as in the thoughtless ransacking of American first nation spirituality by other ethnicities. There is also the risk of unintended conversion if the adopted religion comes to displace that which went before. Alongside such borrowing is the New Age self-assemblage of bits of originally unrelated religious theory or practice. This tends to receive short shrift among theological commentators but those who study religion as an aspect of human activity offer a more sympathetic view, seeing it as creative, joyfully playful and challenging to the old religious institutions.

Not all MRP has belief-based motivation. Sometimes people just want to belong to more than one community, especially at festival times. Crossing religions can arise as a response to social conditions as when Dalits, oppressed in the caste system, took the (theoretical) caste-freedom of Christianity back into their Hindu culture to the frustration of Hindu and Christian establishments alike; and there are cases of religious sharing to express solidarity, as in Ray Gaston's engagement with his local mosque post 9/11. Simple friendship is often bound up with MRP, so that it is unclear which has led to which; they just belong together. MRP can be an unconsidered response to attraction, so that a parallel has been drawn between MRP and love: both are complex, intimate, mutual, a longing for something lasting, with bodily and symbolic aspects, and both work through emotions and ideas together.[16]

To place my own engagement within this swirl of motives and practices, I was pursuing MRP with the hope that this would open my awareness of and responsiveness to God specifically with regard to interreligious relations. It was not "borrowing", despite engaging with *Sikhi* while remaining Christian, because I was approaching *Sikhi* and Christianity as two whole, specific systems without seeking an amalgam, and the research was community-based, unlike the private nature of much borrowing.

While recognizing that there are many writers engaged with MRP and its associated practices I will summarize what is special about this book: it is about the under-reported area of Christian-Sikh relations; it describes that relationship from the beginning and those formative early decisions and experiences, significant in themselves and helpful to anyone considering doing something similar; it deals with my own experience, enabling me to describe the thoughts and feelings that are part of the story; it relies on notes made at the time so it describes confusions and mistakes that often get glossed over in retrospect; it describes my engagement with two active communities which were both aware of what I was doing; and it considers these things in relation to my roles of Church of England priest and interfaith adviser, exploring the tensions that arose.

Religion and difference

Attention to MRP is important because it is one aspect of a much wider cultural shift. The idea of a limited number of coherent historic religions has come under sustained criticism, partly on ideological grounds, with a conviction that we are entering the "Interspiritual Age" and that religious change is part of a move towards a greater world harmony, with present fundamentalisms and nationalisms being seen as eddies in the tide, passing symptoms of resistance. A sociological viewpoint suggests Britain's current situation is that of "superdiversity",[17] a condition observable worldwide and distinguished by a dynamic interplay of all sorts of community and cultural interactions. The study of lived religions is recognizing that religion is made up of ever-changing mixtures of beliefs, practices, experiences, and relationships, which should not be expected to be coherent. Interest in the reality of this unstable mixture is rising, with attention from academic conferences, and it was notable that Kwame Anthony Appiah's 2016 BBC Reith Lectures on the fluidity of personal identity started by paying attention to the religious aspect.

Christian reactions to this vary. Three well-known approaches revolve round hopes of salvation: exclusivists believe salvation rests in Christianity alone; inclusivists see some followers of other religions as "anonymous Christians" drawing on Christian salvation unawares; while pluralists see many religions as having their own saving paths. Other approaches include particularism, which emphasizes the unbridgeable difference between religions with their different languages, core experiences and ideas of salvation; and acceptance, which recognizes that different religious views exist without seeing them as being in competition with Christianity. None of these suggest the need for engagement across faiths, though some accommodate it more easily than others. Relationalism, my preferred approach, prioritizes personal and community relationships, including shared history. Inter-personal and inter-communal relationships are not controlled by or judged under previously held theological positions, but are the reality from which such theories should flow. A well-known practical attempt to deepen interreligious relations is Scriptural Reasoning, where people with a good understanding of their own scriptures meet in small interreligious groups to seek new scriptural insights together. It has been suggested that this could be extended by taking other aspects of religious life as "living texts" to share, but this has not been much developed.

Interreligious prayer

Interreligious prayer is already on the Church agenda. According to a joint declaration from the World Council of Churches and the Vatican it is an "urgent call for a growing number of Christians today, and . . . a matter of concern for all Christians".[18] The Catholic bishops of England and Wales have identified interreligious dialogues of life, action, theological exchange, and religious experience. This last was a call to share spiritual riches such as prayer, contemplation, faith, and methods of searching for God, not so much as ideas to be studied but as ways of living in a positive relationship with others. This approach is described as new to the

Church and recommended only for confident, well-grounded Christians; it should be noted that not all observers recognize this as reflecting the mainstream Roman Catholic position, believing it to be drowned out by anxiety about the threat of syncretism.[19] From the World Council of Churches a consultation was launched in 2014, *Exploring Hybridity, Embracing Hospitality: Towards a Theology of Multiple Belonging*. It led to the publication of a dedicated journal and then a book, twenty-eight articles in all,[20] some of which were more cautious than others, but with an overall trend to call for a hospitable attitude towards an inevitable cultural change: "Religions are not fortresses to be defended but wellsprings of flourishing life!"[21]

A Church of England report from 1992 acknowledged that understanding another faith involves appreciating its worship, but warned that engagement could seem a pretence or a betrayal of one's own faith. Christian participation might mean one thing to Muslims and Jews who would understand that the visitor is from another distinct faith, and another to Hindus and Sikhs, who might see it as confirmation of their own universalist views. Christian ministers were therefore exhorted to caution, remembering the representative nature of their office.[22] Subsequent guidance called for it to be made clear that there is a difference between being present and attentive while prayer is offered from any religion, and actual participation in or assent to that prayer. How to identify this difference is not explained, nor is its significance investigated. More positively a Synod report in 2017 recognized blurred religious identity as a part of the religious setting for much Christian ministry in England, noting that ministry in multi-faith contexts involves meeting people on a spectrum of identity, with clear commitment to a single faith community being only one position among a whole variety of different mixed engagements. While acknowledging that some people find this fluidity a theological problem, attention was paid to the importance of respecting people's self-understanding, even where their self-descriptions challenge traditional categories.[23] This is a rare and welcome example of the confused reality of religious identity being acknowledged without judgement by ecclesiastical authorities.

Individual Anglicans have written a number of practical guides for Christians engaging with neighbours of other faiths. They all in different ways acknowledge the need for openness and vulnerability in ministry, something identified by Roger Hooker and Christopher Lamb in their ground-breaking book of 1986, *Love the Stranger*. As to participating in the prayers of another religion, different conclusions have been reached. Andrew Wingate wrestled with the issue of how to stay faithful while celebrating difference, and over interfaith prayer he concluded that if we are to meet at a heart level we must pray and worship together, even if that involves taking risks. Colin Chapman encouraged Christians to enter friendly dialogue with other faiths, but he left no room for MRP; visiting a mosque should not lead to joining in worship but be a matter of learning and friendship only. Richard Sudworth looked at the wider situation with a prophetic eye, seeing Christian social marginalization as opening up a space in which faith boundaries will be redrawn and the Christian God will act anew. Could this redrawing include shared prayer? He does not say. It is disappointing and perhaps significant[24] that two of the latest books of this type, by Andrew Smith and Tom Wilson, both excellent in their ways, make no reference to prayer together. It may be a difficult topic but it will not go away; 2019 saw the publication of *Interfaith Worship and Prayer*, which has the telling subtitle *We Must Pray Together*, being a line taken from a chapter in the book which argues for worship being shared across religious boundaries. The chapter is written by Christopher Lewis, a former dean of Oxford, who identifies and encourages different types of shared worship: serial events where different religions take responsibility for different sections of the gathering; parallel events where a joint prayer enterprise is undertaken by religions praying separately in their own way (as at Assisi in 1986); rites of passage where one religion acts as host and makes space for another; and genuinely united services, in which the transforming experience of a shared reality binds the participants together.[25] Ray Gaston had previously described sharing in Islamic public worship during the Ramadan fast, a worship he experienced as Islamic in its surrender while remaining focussed on Jesus. The loving openness he was offering expressed the vulnerability for which Hooker and Lamb called.[26] For my part I was exploring that same vulnerability in exposing myself to a new community while remaining open to the judgement of the church in which I had been nurtured.

Religion and identity

Public worship is a sensitive matter, not least because it is where a religious community marks its distinctive identity, something both valued and defended. However, religious identity is also made frustratingly provisional in any worship that points to a divine reality transcending the community's own culture. This tension in worship, both affirming and pointing beyond the gathered religious community, is reflected in interreligious relations. While the blurring of religious identity is seen by some as creating a confused and confusing muddle, potentially dangerous however well-intentioned, others greet it positively as a sign of a new global shared consciousness. These public reactions matter because religious belonging cannot be based on the individual's decision alone; the communities involved must also have their say.

Societies which experience MRP as a normal aspect of life challenge traditional Western Christian ideas of fixed religious identity. As an example, tension surfaced between the Federation of the Asian Bishops' Conferences (FABC) and the Vatican and continued from the 1970s into this century, before FABC's challenge was blunted by the appointment of more conservative bishops under Pope Benedict XVI. A crisis point was reached when the FABC took interreligious dialogue as one of three priorities, along with enculturation and the transformation of political, social and economic life, seeking to show where God is present and active in the everyday rather than engaging in metaphysical argument. This interreligious dialogue involved the sharing of religious practices, something they saw as essential for the enculturation of Christianity, needed to rescue the Church from its colonial past and bring a freedom essential to Christ's kingdom. The Spirit was recognized as present and active in individuals but also in society and history, peoples, cultures, *and religions*.

Peter Phan explored the theology associated with this approach in its welcome of MRB, outlining an "inclusive pluralism". Jesus is seen as the one mediator of God's salvation, but saviour-figures from other religions are thought of as participating in that role, so that MRB is not only possible but also desirable. This was too much for the Vatican and it was denounced as inadequately representing church teaching on the oneness and universality of Jesus as Saviour; the role of non-Christian religions; and (perhaps crucially) the oneness and universality of the Church itself. Phan responded by pointing to the work of the Spirit as a universal "other hand" alongside Jesus; by saying that understanding of other religions must come from engaging with them in Christlike humility; and by affirming that the Church is called to change society rather than be an end in itself. The ecclesiastical authorities have not so far returned fire, but the dialogue demonstrates that what is at stake is not just the Church's approach to other religions but its deeper self-understanding and sense of identity. This sensitivity has been shown up particularly sharply within Catholic structures, but it affects the Christian Church's understanding of itself more widely.

Radical challenges

If Phan faced criticism from conservatives, his framework was also open to challenge from those with more radical views. His approach to dialogue rests on a presentation of different religions as separate blocs, but if religion is seen as a more fluid and multifarious aspect of human existence, worrying about dialogue is just a distraction from the more important business of liberation. A "global practical theology" would arise from interreligious shared responses to the injustices of the world and ecological devastation, responses both contemplative and prophetic but which bypassed declarations of such definitive beliefs as the finality of Jesus. Christianity in this approach is an experience rather than a belief, an experience to be renewed in each culture with no essence needing to be protected. There is also criticism that Phan is over-influenced in his doctrinal concerns by monastic and priestly—male—theological elites, downplaying the everyday mingling which better represents the complex cultures of the majority of women (and men).[27]

The idea of separate religions can be seen as colonialist if from an Asian point of view singular religious identity is the oddity, and I must keep this criticism in mind, because my own bi-religious explorations depend on there being different religions in the first place. Certainly the whole business of religious identity has been high-handedly policed in

Western culture, with *Sikhi* being dismissed in the nineteenth century as a mere combination of Hinduism and Islam. This vetting still goes on: in 2012 the Druid Network was refused membership of the Interfaith Network of the United Kingdom because its presence might cause offence to established members.[28] That policing also affects Christianity, which is often represented in the tame and reasonable forms appreciated by the ruling class, dismissing the anarchic, irrational aspects that give religion much of its vitality.

The idea of separate religions also loses its point if religion as a separate category of human experience itself lacks meaning. Commentators point out that not all communities distinguish between the religious and the secular; others characterize religion in a way too extensive to be useful as a form of etiquette, the rules whereby communities relate. Some understand the category "religion" as not just mistaken but also manipulative, a European distinction exported willy-nilly to the rest of the world. In this view the label "religion" interweaves with issues of resources and power, and takes its place in an overall strategy of giving Westerners the upper hand. Such orientalism is embedded in Western culture and is hard to guard against; I follow two suggested lines of resistance, concentrating on the working together of cultures where they overlap and coexist, and trying to appreciate the concrete experiences of other communities.[29]

My attempt to belong to two religions at once depends on but also problematizes the notion of separate religions, and in its exploration of *Sikhi* (Chapter 5) recognizes the fluidity between what the West identifies as "religion" and other identity-forming factors such as nationality and ethnicity. Reflective practice is inevitably complex and open-ended, but it sheds much-needed light on a discussion in which theoretical descriptions of religion often run into the sands.

Focal points

1. MRP and similar experiences amount to a widespread if controversial activity about which much is currently being written.

2. I have taken MRP as engaging in two enfleshed faith communities and seeking the fullest participation possible in their worship.
3. I have used the description MRP (participation) rather than MRB (belonging), because whether and how participation leads to belonging is a matter for investigation.
4. MRP and similar experiences are part of a wider change in society, welcomed by some as challenging religious divisiveness, and acknowledged by others as a consequence of greater international social mobility.
5. How the churches and individual Christians react to MRP varies, and it is contentious in some quarters, as in some other religions. This tension has a particular focus in attitudes to prayer and worship.
6. Reflective practice is inevitably complex and open-ended, but it sheds much-needed light on a discussion in which theoretical descriptions of religion often run into the sands.

2

Settling in

A normal day in church

There was throughout the fieldwork a heartbeat of worship, week by week. As my research began I was already settled at church, and it was a strange feeling researching a pattern of Christian worship that I had followed throughout my adult life, but it was important to try to capture this "normal" as well as the new engagement. Much MRP involves the continuation of the familiar alongside a more recently adopted practice; both aspects need to be recognized, and both are liable to change.

Beacon Church is a joint Anglican–Methodist church serving an outer estate of eight and a half thousand people just across the boundary from Birmingham in Walsall. The church was consecrated in 1964 by the Church of England before being extended with money from the sale of a nearby Methodist church. Beacon Church is set on a corner, with a forbidding, dark brick wall rising high on the one side, but on the other an entrance hall windowed from ceiling to floor, from which leads a community hall and smaller rooms and kitchens. Down a corridor is the worship area with ninety chairs set in a quarter circle round a dais supporting the communion table, lectern, and prayer desks. There is an organ (unused) to the left, and a concrete font by the door, with children's toys and books to the back right. Warm air heating is noisy but effective, contributing to an inviting area clearly intended for worship though useable in other ways as well.

Anglicans and Methodists worship there as a joint congregation and after twenty years are well integrated, though some carried denominational traditions with them in a relaxed way. A usual congregation of the time was just over thirty, mainly older white British people, the majority of whom were women. The ethnicity but neither the age nor the gender balance matched the local context. A group of about a dozen who had come from the local evangelical church hired a room; they usually worshipped separately but we joined up on special occasions and for coffee. Other regular activities in the building were uniformed children's organizations and commercial activities such as slimming clubs, and there were occasional social and fundraising events. I moved there in October 2013 from another parish, one half-time post replacing another alongside my interfaith role, and was authorized as the congregation's Methodist minister as well as their Anglican priest. Once a month I went on circuit to another Methodist church, and I joined in Methodist as well as Anglican meetings. My worship had a regular weekly routine, and, during the period of my research, I took notes about the services, how I felt and how others reacted.

As soon as I was up and dressed, I would go over my sermon, using the anxiety of the approaching service to sharpen the existing text. The theme would be drawn from set scripture readings, and the hymns already chosen. As I went to church armed with laptop, notes, newssheets, and orders of service I would also take headscarf, recorder, and a copy of some prayers to put in the car for the gurdwara. I would arrive at church at 9 a.m., an hour before the service started, to give me plenty of time to fiddle with the audio-visual equipment, arrange my own material, and generally potter around before other people arrived. I noted how I felt during that time, and there were sometimes hints of weariness: "There in good time but not feeling very inspired. Nervous—why? Thought how marvellous it would be to just run away." These feelings dissipated as the morning progressed, and as I got nearer to retirement. In contrast I noted on another Sunday: "had a feeling that everything was flowing well although I knew objectively I might have expected to be over-tired. Everything seemed to be in God's hand somehow."

On alternate weeks it would be Holy Communion, and there would be a chalice and a rack of individual small glasses filled with non-alcoholic wine, recognizing both Anglican and Methodist traditions. Someone may have provided a loaf, otherwise wafers would be used. Generally the mood was good, and one Sunday I noted church officers "giggling away and generally contented", but there was an occasional hint of irritation:

"She said she was fine, she was just helping out, but it felt there was a bit of significance there." Before the service there was news of members of the congregation who were unwell, or of families or neighbours in difficulties. I noted anxiety over deafness, disappointment over a cataract operation, a husband with skin cancer. Someone had been poorly, and "I felt a bit sheepish about not having noticed he was missing." A request to see me afterwards "left me wondering what was up, and that was in the back of my mind during the service". People were getting refreshments ready for afterwards, but only those with a specific role were around until the last ten minutes when others would begin to gather, most leaving it till the last moment.

As we approached the start of the service, I met in the vestry with the worship stewards and server. Being prayed over in the Methodist manner was calming and focussing, rather than leading the vestry prayer myself as Anglican priests tend to. The congregation stood to sing the first hymn and for communion the server, carrying the processional cross, led me in, both wearing robes. For a Service of the Word I wore suit and clerical collar and entered alone and more briskly. I introduced the theme before continuing according to the day's order of service, the congregation making the responses. I was always aware of the clock at the back of the church and found "timing" to be a concern when I looked back on my notes of the services. A service rarely went without a glitch. There were problems with the microphones, projector, or the music system. Straightforward human errors also cropped up as my concentration flagged, or occasionally from others. I regularly noted my frustration, together with the hope that it did not show too much.

I used doctrinal theology cautiously, noting on one occasion:

> My theme was about the cosmic glory of Christ, and I realized that sounded windy so my punchline was that even words of theology and poetry can matter because they change our attitudes to life and so to each other.

If I preached conservatively that could make me anxious. One Covenant Sunday—a Methodist service of annual recommitment—I preached "at full throttle" but felt uncomfortable encouraging the perfectionism of

Wesley which "seems part of a cycle of high expectations and either failure or hypocrisy". I questioned why I "banged on about it so much", deciding that I was trying to be fair to the Methodist tradition, but was still "guilty of preaching what I didn't believe to please a section of the congregation". Looking back on my themes a number were about persistence, reflecting my personal situation but also that of the congregation. They also showed a liberal tendency: one sermon about faith and doubt claimed that faith in action is more important than theoretical faith. I had spotted a survey about many Christians not believing in the resurrection,[30] and said, "There is little point in trying to argue them into it or saying they should believe in it, but the best thing to do was just to lead a life of faith and hope", and that this was the main test. As I preached there were moments of *hwyl*[31] for me and perhaps for the congregation. Once I read the short verse of *St Patrick's Breastplate*,[32] and it was followed by "a powerful moment with quite a response as everything stilled down; one of those strange moments that catch your throat". The intercessions, led by people on the rota, were all prepared carefully. I relaxed slightly, and my attention sometimes wandered. The peace, during which people moved round church greeting each other, led to a general outpouring of conversation so that it was only by announcing the next hymn that it gradually drew to a close.

For communion, as I went through the Eucharistic Prayer, I did my best to inhabit the present moment and the moment of the last supper at the same time, on one occasion noting: I "realized I was skimming, and slammed the brakes on". This dual engagement still struck me with awe, and that awe carried on into the distribution of communion. I invited anyone "who loves the Lord" to receive, a more open table than I kept as an Anglican but a common phrase in Methodism, and paralleled for me by the open sharing of holy food, *karah parshad*, at the gurdwara. After the Post-communion Prayer, there were notices about future events, then a final hymn, blessing and out.

Conversation at the door and then over coffee included serious family matters: the anniversary of a mother's death; problems at work; a grandchild suffering from depression; an expectant daughter overdue; a disabled daughter's assessment for benefits; a son struck by a virus making him confused and physically unstable. There were issues of community interest: someone working with drug addicts; a phone mast planned on the pavement outside church; the closure of the local Boys' Brigade company. There were emotionally charged trivia: who has access to which cupboards; or, on Easter Day, which church fund should pay for a new urn. Then came those more relaxed conversations which might be accompanied by the admiration of family photographs or playing with someone's dog. It was then I detached myself for the journey to the gurdwara.

There were happy times at Beacon, surrounded by friends, and notes have regular entries such as "lovely atmosphere", "it was an up-beat sort of day", "it was a happy service and people seemed happy with it"; though this was clearly partial in both senses: "afterwards it all seems very good-humoured, but Janice tells me there has been some loud criticism of [. . . a participant in the service] for not doing things right. I hadn't noticed."

My inner reflections were more tentative. One Sunday I journaled:

> Am I just going through the motions like the functionary I sound? I energize myself to try to put some life into the service, but it is only during the sermon and the Communion when we have one that I have any sense of something happening to me. Sometimes that is some sense of conviction and of the significance of what I am saying, a sort of feedback, but more often it takes the form of a love for the people I am with. That is pretty sentimental, but sentiment is important too, if only in spurring me on in my ministry to them. It may not sound much like a relationship with God, but it feels quite a pure one to me, and it cuts through any weariness and futility.

A normal day at the gurdwara

Outside the gurdwara I would pause to record impressions of the service I had left behind at Beacon Church, as trying to do that outside church left me too easily interrupted. I then put on my headscarf (still wearing my clerical collar), took my copies of the daily prayers, the *Ardas*, and walked up to the *Guru Ka Niwas*[33] (GKN) Gurdwara. It has hardly changed externally (it is a listed building) from when it was built in the 1950s for Guest Keen and Nettlefold Engineering; it still looks like an office block and even carries the GKN logo, albeit with a new meaning. It has a lawned area at the front and car-parking along a road that goes round the inside perimeter of the site and opens to a yard at the back. It stands back from a busy dual carriageway and has a new housing estate behind it. There is evidence of the building's new use outside: signs giving the name of the gurdwara in full, identifying it as *Ramgarhia*, a specific social grouping; and an orange flag (*Nishan Sahib*) on a large, orange-swathed pole. As I walk past the pole memories of its dressing return. A new sheath had been put on, censed and perfumed, a new flag attached, and the pole raised:

> They pulled the twine to release the flag and with it had come a cloud of petals, a great many of which fell on me. I was the butt of some good-natured laughter, but people came over to say how lucky it was and began to gather the petals from under me. It had felt a notable bonding experience.

There is nothing special for Sikhs about Sunday morning, but that is usually the busiest time at GKN and other gurdwaras, fitting in with the wider British pattern of public worship. Sometimes there is a special family event, a "programme", going on, something I can[34] foretell by the number of cars outside. If there is a wedding, people will stand outside in their finery. As I continue towards the door I put on my headscarf and remember an issue I had over a hat I was wearing when I enquired about research at a different gurdwara. It was a crocheted hat, easy to pocket, one I had worn for some time as interfaith officer without comment, but as I went to meet the secretary I was told "you had better take off that hat, it's a Muslim hat". A friend later commented that Guru Nanak himself often wore "Muslim" clothes, and that this was an ignorant instruction, but what had struck me most was my abrupt change in status, from respected guest to ill-informed student.

By the gurdwara door is parked a grey car emblazoned with the gurdwara's name. It is used for transporting *Guru Granth Sahib Ji* to people's homes to bless them on special occasions, and the front passenger seat has a special rest for the holy book. Once when they were preparing to go out, they invited me to join them, but I had a wedding to take back at church and missed the opportunity, never repeated. For a couple of years when I went into the gurdwara I used to see the building work on the new hall, but that is now complete. I see the service progressing on an overhead screen ahead. Displayed on the walls are the *Mool Mantra* (the prayer with which *Guru Granth Sahib Ji* commences), a logo for the gurdwara itself, and the Sikh national anthem. Opposite is hand-written, sometimes in English as well as the holy Sikh script of Gurmukhi, the *hukamnama*, the scripture chosen for the day. I slip my shoes off and put them in a locker, wash my hands and go into the worship room, the *durbar*.

I make my donation at the desk by the door as a part of the gurdwara's planned giving scheme, which feels a significant aspect of my opting in, then I move forward to do obeisance before *Guru Granth Sahib Ji*.[35] I bow my head, place a coin in a long box there, then kneel, move forward onto my hands and touch my forehead to the carpet. I stand, bow again, and then sit down on the men's side. The first time I did this was in retrospect important, having merely bowed my head on previous visits to gurdwaras, but I had followed Devsi, my collocutor, and noted, "I hesitated but it seemed a natural thing to do, not the great 'crossing a threshold' feeling I had expected". As to whether it is idolatry, it is worship but that does not necessarily imply the object of worship is divine.[36] For Sikhs the gurus, including *Guru Granth Sahib Ji*, are channels of God's grace but not themselves divine, so I am not bowing down to "another God", leaving aside the issue of whether the Sikh divinity is other to the Judeo-Christian God. All this I might have trotted out as theological justification. The truth is that at the time it felt more liberating than shameful, part of the opening into which Christ has called me.

Despite the soft carpet I am still uncomfortable sitting cross-legged on the floor, sometimes nonetheless keeping it up for over two hours. I was complimented in the early days on sitting upright, encouraging me to try to maintain good posture. I sit cross-legged, but cannot just rest my arms on my knees for long, needing to hug them to keep myself up, and so bending my back. I have recorded stiff knees and hips, even a stiff neck, but at other times it is easier. I noticed the apparent ease with which some maintained an upright position and the sprawling sideways-sitting of others. There is a carpeted bench by the back wall, technically part of the floor, because Sikhs sit in equality on the floor below *Guru Granth Sahib Ji*, though GKN is not strict about this, and chairs often appear as well. Bench and chairs are used by the elderly and the frail, but anyone can support their backs by sitting along the side wall, the committee sitting at the front of the hall. I usually sit in the middle of the floor towards the back, but on quieter days have sat against the wall. Once I stretched out and was told that my legs were too extended, which could be offensive. Other people were doing this, but I was told "you need to know the proper way of doing things". There is less anxiety about physical contact than among white British, so there are unapologetic nudges as neighbours shift positions.[37] About half the men are turbaned; the rest are wearing headscarves. Some wear the tightly pleated turbans of East Africa, others the looser Indian style. Most wear western dress. The women wear headscarves, mainly with the *salwar kameez*;[38] it is rare for a woman to wear a turban here though not unusual in other gurdwaras. There are a few children scattered around, moving between the men's and women's side without tension. Some people are very reverent, others quite casual, chatting or quietly looking at their phones.

The *takhat*, or throne, is central at the front, golden, with Gurmukhi script on it and ornamental lights in the canopy. *Guru Granth Sahib Ji* is covered with and laid on embroidered cloth, often brightly coloured, and behind it stands or sits someone, usually a man, often one of the *granthis* (those paid to read, chant and interpret *Guru Granth Sahib Ji* at the gurdwara), but sometimes a woman or even a child, using *chaur sahib*, the ceremonial fly whisk, signifying reverence of the scripture. In front is the cash box, and donated ornamental cloths, flowers and food. A few people walk clockwise round *Guru Granth Sahib*, removing socks as well as shoes, an additional sign of respect on going behind the *takhat*.

To the right of the *takhat* is a stage for the musicians, designed so that they are sitting lower than *Guru Granth Sahib Ji*. The three musicians, who usually include at least one of the *granthis*, play *tabla*[39] and harmonium, and sing. The congregation sometimes joins in repeated choruses or particularly well known *kirtan*, hymns. Despite encouraging me to learn Punjabi, the secretary said just hearing *kirtan* would be beneficial, and

Devsi said many people there do not understand what they hear, but it is medicine for the soul, healing them without their understanding why. A white Canadian convert to *Sikhi* told me he found *simran*, the repetition of "*Waheguru*",[40] "Wonderful Lord", in a meditative context, an incomparable way of leaving behind the ego. I join in the repetitive choruses, or quietly repeat "*Waheguru*", sometimes alternating with the Christian "*Maranatha*".

One morning I was moved by a solo when every part of the *tabla* was being used with a wide range of tonality and a haunting, irregular beat, like raindrops before the storm. I felt as though my soul was being washed. When I opened my eyes, it was just the drums being tuned, but that move from the tentative and the irregular to the subsequent confident rhythm can still affect me. At other times, I am drowsy and suddenly come to; it's hard to distinguish coming out of a meditative state from simply waking up. Between the songs someone, usually a *granthi* or the secretary, may give a short address, occasionally including a few words of English. People go forward and put money in front of the singers, bowing to *Guru Granth Sahib Ji* as they do so. This may be kept by visiting musicians of note, but most Sundays it goes into the building fund. Sometimes there is a notice encouraging such gifts, but I usually stick at my regular donation.

The prayers, the *Ardas*, invoke institutions and heroes of *Sikhi*, with me following a translation. During the prayers, donations are read out with accompanying prayer requests, and I listen for my name. It is strange that I easily accepted this public announcement of the amount of the donation before the prayers, so different from the church practice of confidential giving. The covers are then removed from *Guru Granth Sahib Ji* and the *hukamnama* is read, the instruction for the day, theoretically at random but always from the more central of the 1,430 pages. In the early months of my attendance I was surprised that, at this high point of the service, people were drifting out to *langar*, the communal meal in the dining hall. After some months the secretary told them to stay, which they did; an unusual example of practice coming into line with what I understood should happen. With the reading the *granthi* sometimes gives a short address, further shortened after people were asked to stay in. The stage secretary then gives out notices and may add a short homily of his own.

Meanwhile one of the *granthis* inserts a *kirpan*[41] in the *karah parshad*, a mixture of wheat flour, sugar and butter warming on a hotplate next to the *takhat*. I originally thought he was just stirring it, but Devsi told me that this modest action has great significance. It is an offering of the food and of those present to the Guru, and as the *kirpan* enters the *karah parshad* so the Guru enters. Five portions are taken out, which may be put before *Guru Granth Sahib Ji*, then distributed as signs of special respect, or mixed back in. It sounded comparable to the breaking of the bread at Christian Communion. *Parshad* is intended to be easy to digest for young and old, a sign of the ease of receiving God's grace; not the identity marker of Christian Communion but to be shared with any visitor. As I receive cross-legged on the floor I am sometimes greeted in English, "Hello John," and sometimes reply "*shukriya*", thank you.

Once after the service I watched an older man come in, speak to one of the *granthis*, have a reading from *Guru Granth Sahib Ji*, and then have something written out and given to him. Later I discovered that I had been watching the naming ceremony, *naam karan*, for his new-born grandchild, in which the first letter of the chosen name is taken from the first letter of a randomly selected reading.[42] I had read about this, and yet had to acknowledge that when it was happening in front of me I did not recognize what was going on.

Devsi and I usually meet as we queue for the meal, *langar*, and others come and greet us, the president often shares a few encouraging words, and the stage secretary offers advice. When I was new, I was sometimes invited to *langar* as I first entered the gurdwara, but preferred to feed afterwards, influenced by the Christian custom of refreshments after services. I noted:

> ... what lies behind these differences, attitudes towards grace and worthiness? Do Christians need to be clean (by fasting and penitence) before communion whereas for Sikhs it is the *simran* itself that makes clean?

It was explained to me that the third Guru of *Sikhi*, Amar Das, made it a rule that anybody who wished to meet him should first eat at the *langar* hall, a way of insisting that all Sikhs ate together, challenging caste and other social divisions. According to tradition even when the great Mughal emperor Akbar came to greet Amar Das the emperor had to sit with the common people for a meal before he was admitted into the guru's presence. I was therefore surprised when the secretary at GKN announced that people really should wait for *langar* until after they had worshipped, not being hungry or having come far as in India. This seemed to be a movement away from Indian roots toward a British Christian practice.

If there is a family programme the hall may be filled with people who have been there for some time. We take metal trays and they are filled at the counter by volunteers doing their *seva*.[43] The food includes yoghurt, a lentil-based spicy food, and some vegetables, again spiced. There are chapatis and rice pudding, and a metal cup of water. Sweets and pickles may appear or even slices of a celebration cake if there is a programme. I sit by Devsi, or with other people I know, usually the younger ones who are happy to converse in English. I may ask what the *granthi* or the secretary have been talking about, or what programme is being celebrated, but talk ranges across British and Punjabi politics, business, news events, gurdwara organization, Sikh tradition and practice, and family news. Occasionally people ask about Christianity, and older members sometimes reminisce about experiences in Britain, India, or East Africa. Others eat quickly and depart without talking, a pattern which I saw with relief was quite normal, not because I had sat there. Women and men usually sit separately, but there are some family groups, and when tables get full women and men mix just to get a place.

If I have time, I help with the washing up. Although this is an important form of *seva*, the men are not always in evidence, but I am happy to join in. There is no language barrier in washing up, it gives an easy opportunity to engage with some of the women, and is important spiritually as a part of my Sikh engagement[44] (with a corresponding worry that in my rush to leave Beacon Church I had become less involved than I was in the washing up there). As I go out a number of senior committee members are counting the money in the *durbar* hall, with older folk sitting chatting at the back. There may be someone reading from *Guru Granth Sahib Ji*, often a woman at that stage. I collect my shoes, perhaps exchange further greetings in the hall, and head back to the car.

I wore my clerical collar at the gurdwara until retirement, and conversation sometimes related to my Christian background: "Someone asked me why Jesus had to die on the cross. I began to run through some of the atonement ideas, but it didn't feel very convincing to me and clearly wasn't to him either . . . " Sikhs have little truck with ideas of atonement for sin, but recognize the place of martyrdom as witness against autocratic power. Can the death of Jesus be understood in that way without emptying the Christian gospel? His death seems (referring back to my vision) to be part of the shadow shape of his humanity *and* light of his glory but pretty inscrutable, and my failure to explain this disturbed me. I felt less dissatisfied with my response to another question:

> A teacher was saying the children have trouble with the idea of healing, and asked what I thought. I said the mystery of prayerful healing is something you only discover when you have been praying for someone and they haven't been healed and on other occasions you have seen miraculous healing, and then you realize it is in God's sovereign hand.

The idea of God's name being a healing thing is important for some Sikhs, so I talked about the disciples' use of the name of Jesus in the Acts of the Apostles (e.g. Acts 2:38).

Variations

Variations at the gurdwara come from special occasions such as weddings. My records show something of the excitement:

> About 11.30, the wedding party started to arrive and the atmosphere began to build. Video men appeared and set up their stands, and a group of men with gold headscarves were clearly in some special position. Children were there and very excited, with the boys in glorious maharaja's costumes and the girls very ornately turned out as well [. . .] The groom arrived in red with a big gold sword, and he had a veil made out of beads

over his face which he kept trying to sweep out of his face but they kept falling down again. He was surrounded by folk and those who had gone through to the *langar* hall drifted back. Then the bride came in, both bride and groom looking a bit anxious as is customary. She was surrounded by a cortege of women, and they sat round the throne including invading the men's side with some of the men sat behind them. The priest gave some instructions in Punjabi, but it was as though no-one had paid any attention, because eventually he said to the bride and groom in English "please stand", so they stood up and there were prayers. Then four of the golden-scarved fellows took up positions on the corners to escort the bride and groom round the *takhat*, and round they went four times between the four prayers with the bride following the groom and holding on to his scarf. There were more prayers, then through into the *langar* hall but the wider wedding party had already been in there for some time so now they were all off somewhere else, leaving it quiet in the hall.

A Western couple I interviewed who had taken *amrit*[45] and had had their religious wedding, *anand karaj*, in the gurdwara told me that as they went through the wedding service, they reflected on a text which they paraphrased: "whatever is on the outside is also on the inside",[46] remembering that the external is the marriage of two people, the internal is the marriage of their minds with God.[47]

Special programmes also mark engagements, significant birthdays, or anniversaries of deaths. The whole gurdwara, especially the *langar* hall, is filled with people, the age range drops and more English is spoken. The women are often in ornate clothing and jewellery,[48] the men in suits, more in headscarves than turbans. The families provide *langar*, a considerable financial outlay, and there may be the singing of "happy birthday" and a cake-cutting ceremony in the *langar* hall. There were other days too where it was busier, including first Sundays of the month when people would gather to hear the text for that month read after the daily *hukamnama*; days of remembrance for the birth or death of a Guru; and the greatest celebration, *Vaisakhi*, marking the foundation of the *Khalsa*. On each of these there would be an added excitement, and talks on the subject concerned. Devsi gave me a calendar so that I could see these holy days and the monthly pattern coming up. For *Vaisakhi* I joined the celebrations in Wolverhampton's West Park (not on the actual date) and was struck as I went past the stage that once I had been up there in my role as Interfaith Officer representing not just the Bishop but all Christians in giving a greeting that seemed to be respectfully received. Now it seemed inappropriate to sit next to the president of my own gurdwara, with people knowing about my stumbling efforts to grasp Sikh practice. I had been reduced to the role of an elementary student, but also felt that I had gained something, and could commend it to other DIFAs, because it relieved the sense of being an imposter that the role of advising on all religions inevitably entails.

Occasionally I would not be able to get to GKN at the usual time. Then I might go on a Saturday, or first thing on Sunday. Unless there was a programme it would be quiet, with just two or three people there. The *prasad*[49] might be fruit and nuts, but there was always something available in the *langar* hall. I would sit more comfortably by the wall, and the few people drifting through were likely to stop to chat. Such times encouraged reflection, as when waiting for the gurdwara to be unlocked at 4.45 a.m. one frosty March morning:

> I stood there, cold at first but then feeling that strange heat that can come if you think yourself warm, listening to the birds and trying to meditate. I remembered the people I had seen kneeling to touch the step on entrance. I was quite worshipful for a few minutes, "*maranatha Waheguru*", as I looked into the CCTV screen showing the worship area. I began to feel cold again as 5 a.m. passed, but the *granthi* came over in his dressing gown, opened the door and went away again. I was there for the procession of *Guru Granth Sahib Ji*, which was brought past me from the *sach khand*, resting place, as I was having a cup of tea in the *langar* hall. There was a block of new flats next door and I had this little fantasy about our living next to the gurdwara and being able to go any time. The fantasy didn't last long because I had to rush off to church.

There was another early Sunday morning when I was there in time to help put out the long sheets that cover the carpet:

> It took twenty minutes. I was worried I might run out of time, but we got it done and when we had finished, they thanked me for my help. There is something nice about doing these practical things of worship together that I remember from being a server at church.

I wondered if I would be invited up to the *sach khand*, and later one of the trustees took me there on a tour of the building:

> Beds with metal, tubular frames, and fairly plain red cloth over them. We thought there were four copies of *Guru Granth Sahib Ji* there, trying to count them under the bedspreads. It reminded me of pyjamas and more soberly of graves.

On that tour we went into the large hall upstairs, currently unusable because of its weak floor. There was a roped off area in the middle to prevent anyone walking over *Guru Granth Sahib Ji* on the floor below and so disrespecting it. There had been some development, but the trustee reflected that because of the floor the money spent on this had most likely been wasted. He said, "You are doing research. You need to know these things." I had heard other criticisms of the management and finances and found there was an openness in sharing these matters that reflected well on the culture in GKN gurdwara, an openness matched by the layout of the building, with its wide windows and open plan (though there were some dingier rooms in the basement). At some gurdwaras the management of large sums of money and different ideas about *Sikhi* can lead to standoffs that last for years, punctuated by court cases and even violence, something off-putting for some Punjabi Sikhs themselves. There was just one serious conflict in the period of my research at GKN which I shall refer to later in as much as it affected me.

There were significant breaks from church routine as well. The insider/outsider distinction was blurred when I was taking services on the Methodist circuit, sometimes leaving me feeling less familiar there than at the gurdwara. To start with I did not take advantage of the freedom available in Methodist worship, but cautiously followed the structure offered in the *Methodist Worship Book,* modelling the content on the examples provided. When I asked people how they had found the service, I got the unexpected reply that it had been a pleasant change, but when I casually asked "In what way, change?" I was left none the wiser. During the first communion on circuit at which I presided,

> I hadn't realized that when people had received communion, they needed dismissal, so everyone stayed at the rail and I asked the steward what to do or say. He said, "You have to dismiss them," and I had to ask, "What do I do to dismiss them?" and so he told me to say a line of a prayer, and off they went.

These things were not always denominational. At one church, the communion table had on it a pyramid with illustrations which didn't seem to have any Christian significance. I remain mystified, never asking what it was or why it was there for fear of causing offence.

There were also less tangible signs of my unfamiliarity with Methodism, as when I was surprised at the circuit superintendent advising me to offer to chair the church council, something automatic in the Church of England. One day we had a coach trip to the Methodist ordination in Liverpool's Anglican Cathedral, similar to my own Anglican ordination in form, but someone explained to me that the new ministers were already presbyters before the service by virtue of a motion in conference receiving them into "Full Connexion", and that the ordination was technically prayer over ministries that had already begun.[50] I had a theological and emotional commitment to the process of ordination that I knew, but my friendship with and appreciation of Methodist colleagues ruled out doubting the validity of this different approach.

Variations also arose when I was away for other reasons, including holidays. I noted an Epiphany service in Birmingham Cathedral: it "spoke to me that following the star is responsive navigating rather than just going in one straight line the whole time". At an Orthodox church in Santorini I went into the church at 10.15 a.m. on a Sunday, but the information I had about a service taking place proved to be wrong. I sat and watched people coming in and going out, including someone with a cassock on who flitted through the church with some linen. There was an animated conversation going on somewhere out of sight. I waited half an hour and then left, noting, "I have considerably less idea what is going on than I have in the gurdwara, but do I still feel more at home here at a deeper level?"

Focal points

1. Engagement with a second religion need not significantly alter how one understands or goes about practising the first.
2. Regular financial donations are an aspect of participation.
3. Threshold actions (e.g. a first prostration before *Guru Granth Sahib Ji*) can feel quite natural in practice despite their theoretical significance.
4. There are bodily aspects to adopting most religions, e.g. discomfort of sitting on the floor. Adaptability to those aspects can affect the sense of belonging.
5. Matching up what one has read with what one experiences is not always easy.
6. The insider/outsider distinction functions within religions as well as between them.

3
Holding it together

Finding my place

Church and gurdwara represent different religions, different groups of people, and meet in different locations at slightly different times. In church I sat on a chair, in the gurdwara on the floor, and my role was completely different. In the church, I understood the language, but in the gurdwara I was relying on others to explain what was being said and sung. In the church the conduct of the service was in my hands and a lot of it in my voice. With that came the security of knowing my role but also anxiety over performance, tied up with my personal and professional integrity. In the gurdwara, I was a guest with few responsibilities, greeted kindly by many, occasionally corrected, but marginal to events, giving a feeling of liberation.

As to similarities, they were on the same morning, public gatherings, in places of worship with a focus—holy table or *Guru Granth Sahib Ji*—in the centre at the front, both with an aisle leading to them. I attended both acts of worship for about the same time, both had a key role for scripture and music, paid worship leaders, teaching on the tradition, intercessions, collections, and holy food, and both concluded with refreshments. Language, sound as well as meaning, and physical posture were significant to both. Although I was much more distracted at church, my underlying attitude, of adoration, intercession, and submission, was the same. To start with I was more aware of myself as an observer in the gurdwara, but while the act of reporting on my time in church developed my awareness of my observer status there, in contrast, as I became more familiar with the gurdwara, my sense of being an outsider there reduced.

Language had the potential to be a major barrier in my engagement with *Sikhi*. I applied for an adult education course in Punjabi at the Library of Birmingham, only to have that cancelled for lack of support. At one point a gurdwara trustee introduced me to a woman who was thinking of opening a Punjabi class for children at the gurdwara, and she invited me to attend. It was the first such class in my time at GKN, despite their availability in other gurdwaras, and was a most welcome proposal. Devsi later gave me a course that he had prepared for health workers, and I also learned to transliterate the Gurmukhi script, but I had difficulty distinguishing the Punjabi tonalities so that even the few common phrases I learned were not easily understood. I was grateful to those who spoke to me in English, and consoled by the difficulties Punjabi people themselves have with the *Guru Granth Sahib Ji*, which has passages from a number of different languages ("It's really difficult, not just like 'thees' and 'thous' in Shakespeare"), and by the preference of many younger British Punjabis for English ("they only hear Punjabi when their grandmothers are telling them off"), including a third who would prefer gurdwara worship to be in English.[51] One of my interviewees told me:

> I go to the... [gurdwara] because I am Sikh primarily, but having been born and brought up in England, my communication skills are geared more around English than Punjabi my ethnic tongue... when I go to the Sikh gurdwara I don't understand it all, when I go to church I do... I find myself closer to God when I'm in a Christian church than when I'm in a Sikh gurdwara.

Other DIFAs have difficulty learning Punjabi, and British converts can find it hard, even those who marry Punjabi Sikhs, though one *Amritdhari*[52] convert commented:

> Whether it's language or culture, any of these things, for me they haven't been a barrier. Yes, very challenging when you go to the services and they are all in Punjabi but I always have the company of people who if I need something translated they will translate it.

For a long time, there were to be no classes at GKN;[53] the project drifted into abeyance and my Punjabi remains minimal. People were nonetheless talking freely with me at the gurdwara, even beginning to discuss sensitive matters, but it was as a guest and a student I was finding my place:

> It is something of a Copernican revolution as you place yourself in someone else's world. I feel I am held in planetary orbit, maintained at a correct distance by the gurdwara, correct for them as well as for me. It's not like if you go to church, and you'll have someone trying to persuade you to go on the coffee rota or be confirmed or go to an Alpha class, there isn't an obvious progression, but neither is there any attempt to repel me, people are very friendly and welcoming. The expectation of the community seems to be that I will just stay as I am, but there is a bit of me that feels, from the point of view of the research and personally, "Is that it?"

In dialogue with Mark Stobert, my reflection partner, I was challenged to push the boundaries: (Stobert) "Would it be costly or life-enhancing to knock that orbit a bit, if you ventured to get closer in or change the orbit? It's almost like action research, 'what would happen if . . . ?'" This orbiting was not a serene progress, but one of contrasting pressures: "When it came to the putting away [after the washing up], I was the one who knew where things went with others turning to me, which was a nice feeling, being on home ground," but days later: "The secretary came in and I mucked up the greeting '*waheguru ji ka kalsa*', '*waheguru ji ki fateh*', which was embarrassing. I feel awkward with him at the moment." My academic reviewer picked up on this. It seemed to him quite a bumpy oscillation, between feeling really in at one moment and really out the next. I suggested an image of these being the gravitational forces that held me in position. Overall I found being marginal an enjoyable change from my central role in church life. Whether I would have enjoyed it as much if my whole life had been marginalized I did not know, though as retirement continues I am finding there is nothing to fear. In any case the stasis was illusory: in the coming months relationships would develop and change.

The difficulty over language presented a barrier, but there were other factors working, sometimes unexpectedly, to enmesh my two religious practices together: "I noticed how much I appreciated *karah parshad*. I'm on a diet, and this is the only sweet thing I have had all week except a bit of Christmas cake, two religiously related moments of sweetness in an otherwise bland week." Mine was a bodily engagement with the two religions, as this and the pains of sitting cross-legged indicated. My body was shaping and being shaped by the experience as I shuttled back and forth, engaging in a regular learned physical entanglement which had become a habit. As my mind sought a workable cross-religious relationship my body was already acting it out.

Similarities and differences of belief

Although I am describing an experience rather than comparing beliefs, how I managed differences of belief was a part of my engagement. Similarities between Christianity and *Sikhi* as I experienced them were: the centrality of God's grace, with the *mool mantra* referring to it; and the uselessness of humankind acting through their own wilfulness (*manmukh*) being a main theme of *Guru Granth Sahib Ji*. The loving relationship between God and follower is clearly there in both, though balanced in both by a sense of mystery and awe in the face of the divine. There are similarities in ethics: concern for the vulnerable, service to others, willing self-sacrifice, honesty, and mutual support; and, for a Protestant, there was a recognizable strain of anti-religiosity in both religions. I was happy to recognize these similarities but never took them as signs that both religions are at heart the same, as regularly encouraged to by Sikh friends. They were signs of sufficient similarities to allow mutual understanding, respect and enjoyment, but differences remained.

A clear difference I had felt between Christianity and the Vedic religions was over reincarnation as contrasted with the individualism and uniqueness of resurrection, something that seemed to indicate a different way of understanding the very nature of existence. A convert from *Sikhi* to Christianity has described herself as being propelled by fear of reincarnation,[54] but *Sikhi* is not itself tied to reincarnation. It teaches that constant recollection of God's grace breaks the cycle of birth and death, *awagaun*, and liberation, *mukti*, is then attained; and regards any interest in a continued individual entity as unhealthily self-centred.

On the Christian side, belief in the pre-existence of the soul (and thus reincarnation) was banned in 553. However, many Christian leaders have advocated reincarnation since, including Cardinal Mercier and Leslie Weatherhead, a renowned president of the British Methodist Conference. I was particularly interested that Bishop Hugh Montefiore, who ordained me as priest, was one such, believing that reincarnation is not only possible but probable, and fits with the Christian understanding of God's nature through its continuing possibility of redemption. He was also impressed by the evidence of people recalling their former lives.[55] A significant minority of contemporary Christians, 24 per cent of American Christians, 28 per cent of British Christians, claim to believe in reincarnation.[56] The anthropologist Martin Stringer recorded an Anglican church group in Manchester talking about prayers for the dead where one of the participants happened to say that they liked the idea of reincarnation and nearly everyone went on to agree, saying that reincarnation seemed more likely than going straight to heaven.[57] One of my interviewees who had become a Sikh without repudiating her Christian background had been drawn towards *Sikhi* initially because reincarnation is more merciful and more just than one life followed for many by the flames of hell.

From the other direction the disconnection between Sikhs and resurrection theology is not quite total. The poem *The Man Who Never Died*, written by a Sikh from within Sikh tradition, offers an interpretation of the Christian gospel that demonstrates the spiritual view of resurrection. This is distinct from statements about the resurrection of the body, but the spiritual view is seen by some as coinciding with the earliest Christian understanding.[58] It was becoming harder to pin down the differences of belief between these two monotheistic faiths.

The main issue was not primarily about conflicting beliefs but about conflicting loyalties. As a Christian I acknowledge the exclusive claims of Jesus as presented by tradition and scripture: "No one comes to the Father except through me" (John 14:6); "There is no other name under heaven ... " (Acts 4:12), but this was balanced by the experience of invitation I had received in the gym in 2007, and a more long-standing discomfort at the way that tradition is presented. I am similarly aware that *Sikhi*, despite its respect for other religions, draws on the tradition of gurudom, a unique relationship, and has in its history a demarcation from Hinduism that expects that Sikhs do not owe allegiance to any other religion.[59] I would need to address this.

Managing difference

One way of dealing with these tensions is universalism, the claim that all faiths have a shared underlying truth. The problem with this is the suggestion that if one can identify behind different religions some common factor as the true meaning of them all, that meaning is inevitably cloudy. Reaching for this one true meaning sucks the sense of the ultimate out of individual religions, and with it their authority and some of their attraction. Another way of dismissing difference is to lose the whole notion of multiplicity in the transcendental, a significant element of Sikh philosophy: *Guru Granth Sahib Ji* begins with the words *Ikk Oan Kar*, "One Being Is". To lose the distinction between self and other leads to unity with all existing things and with God, and the issue of loyalty melts away. There is no "self" making the choice between religions nor are there two separate religions. I was sometimes aware in retrospect of losing myself in meditation, but I drew back from this unified state. This hesitation formed a focal point in my guided reflection sessions.

> (Stobert:) "I guess they [Jesus and Nanak] will continue to be separate until you transcend them."

I demurred: "That is a strange thing to do to your guru."

> (Stobert:) "Why wouldn't they want you to become your own person, a Guru or a Christ?"

We explored this a number of times, and it was exhilarating, but I found I was still engaging with a Jesus and a Guru "out there". My personal relationship with Jesus had been reinvigorated by the vision, and I was developing an awareness of the personality of Guru Nanak that was leading me to seek a relationship with him as well.

By rejecting universalism and transcendentalism I was still faced with a conflict of beliefs and loyalties, but this was not as disconcerting as might be expected; contradictory religious impulses can live together in the heart. How do people deal with inconsistent ideas and beliefs, logical, cultural, or arising from experience, and how do they reduce the resulting inconsistency, the dissonance? Katherine Rand carried out research among a number of people engaging in MRP in Indonesia and came to the conclusion that they had no problems over internal conflict but that their difficulties came with managing the expectations of others around them. Continuing psychological research in this area suggests that more generally, dissonance in itself is not difficult for people to live with. Specific adverse consequences are needed to generate sufficient discomfort to give the impetus for change.[60] There are some adverse consequences for me in adopting two different belief systems, internal incoherence and being open to criticism from others, but there are also the attractions of holding novelty and familiarity together, and an enlarged social circle.

This capacity to live with cognitive dissonance is particularly relevant to faith issues for it is required within any developed religious belief system. Christians are trained in this acceptance by the three-and-one doctrine of the Trinity and by the claim that Christ is fully God and fully human and yet of one nature; and more down-to-earth research on religious attitudes in Birmingham showed that people simultaneously held contrasting views of the necessity of baptism depending on whether they are speaking generally (more lax) or about their own family (more strict).[61] Sikhs also have issues over which they must hold contradiction together, such as the belief that God has attributes and at the same time that he does not, his presence in adoration and his utter transcendence, *nirgun sargun*. Behind these examples the opposites of divine immanence and divine transcendence are maintained in relationship in both Christianity and *Sikhi*, and that is a more radical dissonance than anything between the faiths. If these contradictions within faiths can be dignified as paradoxes or elements in a dialectic, then so can differences between faiths.

Hesitations

My leading of worship did not seem to be changed by engagement with *Sikhi*, but there were a few moments of anxiety[62] and of comparison. When preaching about baptism I reflected on: "the work on identity I am doing with the Sikhs, remembering [the family from a Sikh background at a Christian church] who will take Communion but not be baptized." I noted about one member of the congregation at Beacon Church that:

> Amy[63] feels there is something missing with no outward reverences. I still find it hard not to bow to the table (which would be a bit hyper-Anglican and show offy in this setting) and the Sikh obeisance in the gurdwara has become important to me.

I noted that before the service "I had time to meditate and used '*maranatha Waheguru*',[64] and I don't think that felt odd, it felt fine really." I rarely referred to interreligious experience in my preaching, though once I recalled a Sikh convert to Christianity "and how she had reminded me of the new life of Christianity", and one St George's Day I preached that "identity can either be formed by who we are opposed to or who we have links to" and noted "connected with my research".

During the first six months of my attendance at the gurdwara, I did have moments of unease. Early one Easter morning, attending the gurdwara at 6 a.m., before church, I sat in the car outside to finish listening to a reflection on the radio: "Why are you looking for the living among the dead?" This call to focus on Jesus left me feeling chastened, adrift, but the mood did not last when I went into the gurdwara:

> The sun was coming in through the windows and the white robes of the *granthi* were hanging on the coat stand. It reminded me of the light from the empty tomb and the Easter garments hanging on the cross. There was a bed at the back, I guess for those taking shifts on reading through the *Guru Granth Sahib Ji*. It was white, folded back, like grave clothes.

Regret sometimes struck me while in church:

I was talking about the work of the Holy Spirit and found I was speaking with conviction, and then felt sad. It was sadness at what I was leaving behind and I suddenly thought "why am I mucking this all around?" Anyway the feeling didn't last long, it was a sunny day.

I had lurking at the back of my mind the feeling that there was something faithless about what I was doing with *Sikhi*, but when I thought about it later I couldn't really earth where that guilt was coming from.

In July 2016, I preached about finding one's true identity in Christ but reflected, "How does that tie in with my engagement (and confusion?) with *Sikhi*?" This was the last reference to this type of anxiety in my journal, which might suggest that for the final year the tension was resolved or suppressed as the new practice became established, but even towards the end of my research the issue of betrayal still proved to be on my mind. The Church of England report *Multi-Faith Worship?* had asked whether such engagement can be a betrayal of one's own faith,[65] and I realized this suggestion was still troubling me when I found I had drawn from a bookshop shelf Avishai Margalit's *On Betrayal* (2017).[66] He describes betrayal as a matter of ethics, applying within pre-existing relationships, contrasted with morality which gives rise to general duties. Betrayal is ungluing the glue of thick relationships, something which is worst where relationships are thickest. "Thickness" suggests many layers of obligation as well as the strength of ties, and Margalit takes family and friendship as the strongest, of which other forms of betrayal including apostasy—betrayal of the religious community—and idolatry—betrayal of God—are reflections. The offence of betrayal need not arise from an intention to cause hurt. Recklessness can be just as painful, as when a married person has an affair they hope but fail to keep secret.

My MRP has not been secret, as I had been careful to get the agreement of bishop, congregation, and the gurdwara involved, but while expressing a continuing loyalty to Jesus and to the Church I now have another loyalty as well, to *Sikhi*, which could be viewed as recklessly ungluing the ecclesiastical mortar. Like the spy Klaus Fuchs, whose citizenship of the UK seemed compatible with working for the Soviet Union when it was a wartime ally, could contradictions emerge as circumstances change, meaning I was already delusional in believing my two loyalties to be compatible? Christians have not been persecuted by Sikhs, a context which would problematize a dual loyalty, but Sikhs have suffered at the hands of "Christian" states and individuals; and it was also awkward explaining myself to *Sant Nirankari, Ek Niwas* and *Ravidassi* friends, with their varied experiences of Sikh hostility. The possibilities for MRP vary between different religious groupings and vary with time and place as the social context changes.

I had to acknowledge that my relationship to the Christian Church has all the hallmarks of a thick relationship, incorporating friendships, loyalty confirmed on oath to a series of bishops, my family's church engagement, the provision of my livelihood, and my world view. That thickness makes it a possible scenario for betrayal, a disloyalty made worse by underlying ingratitude. I have much for which to thank the Church and carry Thomas Traherne's aphorism with me: " . . . all the business of Religion on GODS part is Bounty, Gratitude on ours . . . ".[67]

This unease would be a problem for pursuing MRP myself or for suggesting to fellow DIFAs that MRP is a valuable experience unless it is possible that unpicking the model of absolute singular devotion is not a threat to the Church but a potential blessing. Single loyalties are certainly helpful in establishing social control, public profile, and *esprit de corps*, but Susan Katz Miller puts the case for recognizing religious duality in families as bringing other benefits to the faiths concerned.[68] These benefits are not institutional but spiritual, a claim which requires theological justification.

Jesus Christ and Guru Nanak established a channel of teaching through Peter and Guru Angad respectively to ensure their word and work continued after their mortal presence, but this is not the same as their seeking to establish new religions. For Evangelicals, it is a commonplace understanding that following Jesus is not a religion, something also explored by radical Protestants like Dietrich Bonhoeffer. One way of understanding Jesus' teaching ministry is as the reclamation of the Father God from the religious authorities; and Guru Nanak's declaration that "there is no Hindu, there is no Muslim" is usually understood as a challenge to the whole notion of religious identity before God;[69] he criticized religiosity so strongly that Christians have recognized parallels between him and his contemporary, Martin Luther. Gerald Hughes reminded Christians that "God breaks down in us all our comforting prejudices and false securities, religious and secular. This is very painful for us, but it is the pain of rebirth."[70] Maybe to truly follow Jesus or Nanak is not to give succour to religious institutions but to unsettle them in the light of the kingdom, and this disruption is an act of higher loyalty. The disgrace of the churches' handling of child abuse has made clear that protection of the institution must never be put ahead of truth-telling and attending to people's actual experience, that which is being called for here. If such unsettling can be spiritually beneficial to church and *sangat* with its re-emphasis on the otherness of God, I avoid charges of apostasy by turning to the examples of Jesus and the gurus themselves.

As to idolatry, the jealousy of monotheism parallels the lover's demand for a unique relationship, and Margalit affirmed love as a relationship between two people, seeing a three-way relationship in that context as inevitably treacherous. However, he did acknowledge that friendship, the model being explored here, does not demand exclusivity but can be expanded to the mutual benefit of all concerned. Most importantly this investigation is not an attempt to replace God with something else, which is the basis of idolatry, or to supplement a perceived lack, but to catch the experience of the one God unawares, to be surprised by God afresh. Bringing Indian and Semitic religions into relationship can move theology forward (as in *Sikhi* itself), giving a new field of meaning to one's own experience, but while the believer's experience of the religions is refreshed the One God is not disparaged in the process.

Focal points

1. Language difference is a very significant cultural barrier, but language sometimes presents difficulties within a religious tradition, and the barrier is not absolute.
2. The bodily aspect of engagement signified I was the same person at both places of worship despite experimenting with different identities and beliefs. The same body carried out learned

performances at both and moved between the places of worship, knitting the two experiences together.

3. Despite the encouragement of Sikh friends, I could not say differences of belief were insignificant as in the universalist position, nor adopt the dismissal of difference itself in line with transcendentalists.
4. Nonetheless difference was surprisingly easy to live with, bearing out that cognitive dissonance is not a problem unless there are other adverse consequences. Acceptance of such dissonance is required within religious systems as well as between them.
5. The issue of loyalty is difficult and may be exacerbated by historical, cultural, and political factors. In the early days there was occasional nostalgia for the first religion alone.
6. Loyalty to religious institutions can be trumped by loyalty to the teaching and example of founders who may be radically critical of those institutions and point beyond themselves to the one God.

4

Challenges

Obtaining permission

Alongside these times of anxiety, I faced some practical challenges, challenges that had begun before the arrangement was made with GKN. There was to be nothing clandestine about my MRP, so the initial need was to find a gurdwara where I would be permitted to conduct this experimental participation and to write about it afterwards. The first attempt was to end in complete failure. As I took this in, I tried to trace where things had gone wrong. To start with things seemed fine. I had been attending the gurdwara for six weeks, and had always been greeted warmly, with people happy to speak with me and explain what was going on. I had even started making field notes in the expectation that the committee would give their approval.

I had been discussing the research since having the initial idea with L, a committee member at the gurdwara and someone I knew through organizing interreligious football matches together. He thought it would be OK and took me to see the General Secretary, an older, rather twinkly man who was very pleasant. The meeting was friendly and business-like, and I left with him copies of a research summary and a letter seeking the committee's agreement. A delay until next month for the committee to meet was a nuisance, but there was nothing to be done about it. Thinking back though there were three clouds on the horizon: first, a warning that the committee itself was divided between the old guard and a younger generation; second, that I had not approached the education officer, S, whom I knew but whose role I had not appreciated as being connected with this; and third, a flat rejection of my offer to come and meet the committee as "not necessary".

I rang S, and we agreed to meet the following Sunday. I apologized for not contacting him in the first place, but he seemed unconcerned and was very gracious about it. He said that he didn't think there was likely to be a problem with the committee, but that it would be important for the approval to be formally minuted, so that it was on record for the new committee being elected in May. I felt fairly confident the research would be agreed. The next weekend I saw S again: "There are a few questions the committee is asking." This surprised me as I didn't think it had met yet; had there been some sort of impromptu gathering? He said we needed to book a time to discuss these questions, and we arranged a meeting for the Thursday evening. The need to do this felt odd, uncomfortably formal. The meeting started in the dining hall and was relaxed enough, with enquiries about the family and each other's children. The conversation meandered on, but it seemed that I would need to raise the issue of the committee's questions myself, so eventually I did. S suggested we go to the classroom upstairs.

It was quiet and dark, with movement-sensitive lights flickering on and off as we passed by. We entered a large classroom, and S chose where we sat carefully, trying a couple of tables before we eventually settled, with a nervousness that was contagious. In his hand he had the documents I had provided, and I could see they were heavily overwritten with comments. The questions began with the issue of language: "How will you manage without knowing Punjabi?" We had quite a lengthy conversation about it. We talked about the translations available, including those on the screens at that gurdwara and those I had at home. I told him that I was studying Sikh scripture and had received an offer to teach me some Punjabi; I added that I was looking out for Punjabi classes, but there did not seem to be any at the gurdwara. S confirmed that the classes they once ran no longer take place. I said that I had noticed that much of the conversation— about half—in the dining hall was in English. This discussion of language petered out rather than reaching any conclusion . . .

"We have some very clever people on the committee, doctors, lawyers, and so on, and they wonder how you are qualified to do research into Sikhism." I explained that I was working on a reflective piece describing the experience of deepening engagement across religions rather than a dissertation on *Sikhi* as such, and I mentioned my academic qualifications.

He said: "We realize Christian ministers are all very learned." It didn't sound sarcastic but had a tone behind it that I could not identify, perhaps embarrassment at my defensiveness. Again the subject seems to have run its course without any conclusion . . .

"When your research is finished, what happens then?" I would spend some time writing about and reflecting on my experience with the eventual aim of publishing something. Committee members would be welcome to comment on a draft beforehand, but it must be my own work based on my experience. S said, "I thought that would be so." Then came what seemed the nub of the conversation: "We can't commit the gurdwara to such a project before the election of the new committee in May next year." I explained that a seven-month delay would be a serious setback, and S said rather sadly, "I thought that would be so." I was most welcome to keep attending and asking about things but not to begin any formal research yet, and, in view of the delay and the uncertainty about the outcome in May S concluded, "I think it would be better to try somewhere else." Considering how tentatively he had proceeded throughout the discussion, the bluntness of this verdict was a shock for which I was unprepared, but there was no mistake. "Perhaps you could pursue it with another faith or with Sikhs in another town, but not here." Discussion continued in a pleasant if rather sad tone, with repeated assurances that I would be most welcome to spend time there whenever it suited me, but my mind was now elsewhere. We parted at 8.45 p.m. after a conversation of over three hours.

This was a painful experience, a personal and professional rejection, and, as someone secure at the time in my social, religious, and family situations, an unfamiliar experience. I felt disappointed, part resentful and part ashamed, with little of the peaceable humility Christian faith—or even a general spiritual maturity—should bring. Perhaps medics and lawyers did not grasp the nature of reflective practice; was I a victim of discipline discrimination? I felt sheepish that I had not foreseen this and that I still did not fully understand what was going on. Why did the change of committee loom so large? Now I felt like an innocent—but clueless—bystander rather than misunderstood. The invitation to carry on attending seemed genuine and the question about what would happen with my findings had been presented casually, but was this, after all, the real problem? Or was there a deeper, more instinctive element? Was I no longer fitting into the familiar role of "guest"? I was later told by two different sources within the gurdwara that a significant problem was that no-one had the confidence to guide me through the sort of exploration I was intending.[71] Was it less my ignorance than my attempt to gain in knowledge and experience that was unsettling? If so, what did that say about boundary issues? Even S himself found a translation of the Sikh scriptures helpful, so was the language barrier less a practical difficulty than a social boundary? Could my quest be unsettling their own sense of identity?

Then there was *my* identity as a white Christian Englishman. Was lack of Punjabi seen as a lack of respect for the culture I was seeking to investigate? Gurmukhi, the distinctive Punjabi script, is a holy language developed by Guru Angad for the very purpose of writing scripture. Perhaps I was seen as guilty of deep-rooted imperialist insensitivity. And perhaps I was guilty. The Tower of Babel (Genesis 11:1–9) showed the breakdown of a universal language as the response of a jealous God to humankind overreaching ourselves.[72] My research could be regarded as just such an attempt at self-transcendence, trying to see the world from another worldview than my own, an impious arrogance, perhaps sensed by whoever had turned me down. As I pondered these things discussions continued. My original contact, L, tried to get the decision changed before developing a growing awareness of difficulty.

I decided to embark on a Plan B, and turned to Devsi, who told me not to worry and started negotiations at his own gurdwara. Discussions there also moved slowly, but after several weeks I was invited to attend a committee meeting. A dozen middle-aged or elderly men were sat round a table. I explained the project, its limited life-span and positive intention, and tried to make clear that I was not carrying out an objective investigation of *Sikhi* but wanted to share in and reflect on the experience of worshipping in two religions. Devsi acted as my advocate, stressing that it would publicize the gurdwara and help to make *Sikhi* better known. After some questions I withdrew, but they soon called me back and agreed to the research, exchanging pleasantries as the president signed a letter signifying their approval. I was aware that Devsi's line of argument had put me under an obligation towards them, and was starkly aware that obtaining permission had been dependent on friendship; the very thing I had characterized as an insufficiently firm foundation for interreligious relations had turned out to be essential to the establishment of my research.[73]

As for getting permission from the Church, Bishop Clive was supportive from the start, and this was especially significant because he was not some remote authority figure but my line-manager, who took a close interest in the interfaith work, and he was allowing me to spend some of the limited time I had available for interfaith work on developing this approach. As to the local church, after informal conversations I put my request to church council, explained what I was about, and then left the room. They gave their consent to my writing about my experience with them and to my engagement with *Sikhi*, and some showed continued interest and encouragement throughout the research. I told the archdeacon what was going on, so that she could assure herself that no misgivings were arising in the congregation as the research progressed. As it happened, I knew of no anxiety on their part at any stage.

Pattern of life

I was not trying to lead the life of an *Amritdhari*, and so did not become vegetarian or teetotal, as only 27 per cent of Sikhs are the former and 37 per cent the latter, but I did cease eating beef throughout my fieldwork, along with 56 per cent of Sikhs, something that needed explaining to friends and family.[74] It was only when Devsi corrected this that I realized Amritdhari need not be vegetarian, although all food in the gurdwara is vegetarian. It was generally kindly received, but sometimes with a sense that I was being eccentric. I was upset when a close family member asked whether I was still a Christian, but we talked about it, and she reassured me she was confident I was, "but a bit different because you're not judgemental". Taking *langar* meant that I was too full to share in Sunday lunch, which broke with what had been a centrepiece of domestic life: "In prioritizing my social contact at the gurdwara I am breaking a social contact with the immediate family." Being at the gurdwara also made me late for special occasions with the wider family, birthdays and the like, which were often celebrated by a meal out. Family was accepting, but I was having to apologize for the consequences of my engagement with *Sikhi*.

There were other decisions to be made, including over dress. I wore a headscarf in the gurdwara and when I was engaging in *seva* with other Sikhs, but continued as normal elsewhere. At the first gurdwara I was sorting through the headscarves provided when someone offered to tie a turban on me, but there were no suitable cloths available. I was touched by this friendly gesture, but wondered what people in the gurdwara would have thought, and then what it would have been like to wear it throughout the day. I found later that the practice of putting on a turban just to go to the gurdwara was disparaged among Sikhs ("like wearing a hat"), and wearing it continually would have been insensitive in my Christian ministry, especially when dealing with occasional contacts as at funerals. However, when I attended an event marking the fortieth anniversary of Sikh bus drivers being allowed turbans, there was an invitation to non-Sikhs to wear turbans themselves as signs of solidarity. A couple of Sikh friends offered to tie one on me, and I accepted. With their support I decided to wear it for the rest of a busy day, round Wolverhampton, in a Hindu temple, and on Birmingham University campus. I was aware of the discrimination against the turban that we had been hearing about at the celebration, but my own aroused little reaction, even combined with a clerical collar. Only my academic adviser showed any unease. Before I explained the background, he was worried that I was taking an overdramatic stance to unnaturally force the pace of my research. Overall the day of wearing a turban felt like dressing up, raising the issue of pretence. There was no deception of others intended or likely, but was there self-delusion? I was aware of a sense of playfulness, shared with those who had put the turban on me, and wondered how appropriate that was on a day when the fight to be able to wear it was being celebrated. "Playing at it" was an accusation that could be levelled at my whole Sikh experience, and how accurate it would turn out to be depended on how things progressed.

Some photographs were taken, and I entered one for an *Images of Research* exhibition at the university. It aroused interest and was enquired after as an image for an anti-discrimination campaign on campus, though not eventually used. At the exhibition launch, where it was displayed with a brief description of my research, a student from Jordan said no such experimentation could be considered in her country, where religious identity was marked on all government paperwork and maintained by rigid social structures. The picture was later used on the front page of the Lichfield diocesan website, suggesting the ease with which the diocese accepted my explorations.

Another decision to be made concerned my participation in Holy Communion. At Beacon Church I had communicated with both Anglican wine that included alcohol and Methodist non-alcoholic wine, marking my participation in both denominations. However, it was taboo to attend the gurdwara after taking alcohol and, although it was unlikely to be detected, I was uneasy that I was abusing their hospitality and not preparing myself spiritually. It was an easy change to make, unnoticed I think in church, to take just the non-alcoholic wine, but when I mentioned it to my reflection partner, he questioned me. I had received Anglican Communion since I was thirteen, and now I was throwing that over without much thought, adapting my Christian practice to meet Sikh requirements, but not the other way round. I was stimulated by this challenge, but rejected it. I was happy to take communion without alcohol whenever I was on Methodist circuit, and had long been moved by the description of Bishop Leonard Wilson giving a communion of rice while interned in Singapore. As to the wider point, with Christianity being my base it was inevitably my Christian practice that would change. There were plenty of examples (e.g. not wearing a turban) of Sikh practice being moderated in deference to my Christianity. But I had made the change without much thought, and needed to have this pointed out.

As time went on, I faced challenges to my engagement with GKN gurdwara from temptations to move to other non-Christian bases. On one early-morning visit to GKN, there was an enthusiastic visitor there who invited me to go to another gurdwara with a *granthi* who spoke good English, and I did visit a couple of times. It was nearer home, the *granthi* was friendly, a Punjabi convert from Christianity, and the teaching included English passages ("whoso remembers me lovingly, his insides start singing"). I was told decisions were made by the whole congregation together "on the principle of love", which had a Quaker-like attractiveness. On the other hand, the main time of worship was 5 a.m., and they were followers of a Canadian education programme, *Gobind Sarvar*, the standing of which in the Sikh community I could not judge.

Another temptation to move concerned *Ek Niwas* temple in Wolverhampton. The priest, another Punjabi, had had a vision from God calling all religions together and had established a temple which included *Guru Granth Sahib Ji* alongside images of many religions and beliefs, including the Sacred Heart of Jesus, the Buddha, a first-nation American, Neptune, and a wizard. Sikhs had attempted to get it shut down, objecting to *Guru Granth Sahib Ji* being kept in such company, and the scriptures were removed, though the empty throne is still there, as are images of the gurus, and some hostility remains. I went there as part of my interfaith work, a visit that itself led to Sikh complaint. As I was going round this interreligious setting established in the face of opposition, I felt some of its attraction and sympathy for those involved, and I found some of the priest's stories very touching. Once he told me of his own visitation from Jesus, which had come about when the priest's car broke down as he set off to travel to Leeds. Jesus told him to go instead to the German war cemetery in Cannock, but he objected that his own guru had told him he must make the journey to Leeds. Jesus smiled and said, "Start the car then!", but the car would not go. Jesus left, but the priest's own guru appeared and told him to do as Jesus had said. The car then started, and he went to the cemetery where he was told to pray for the release of the souls of those buried there, souls he saw rise from their graves and go free.

But I did not transfer. My project was not headed towards a homogeneous blending, I could not accept the message of the temple that all religions were essentially one, and I would have exchanged relating to two major world faiths, Christianity and *Sikhi*, for relating to a small sect rejected by both. The deciding factor in both cases was that I had a loyalty to GKN gurdwara, to people with whom bonds of friendship were developing, now being reinforced by habit.

Challenges from colleagues

Other challenges came from within the Christian community. While I was doing my research, I did not shy away from those in my own circle who objected, but neither did I actively seek confrontation with strangers, a reticence which the publication of this book may remedy. I was surprised that none of the converts I interviewed, Sikh to Christian or Christian to Sikh, criticized my double-sidedness, as I had expected them to be the most clear on the need to make a choice. I had not taken into account that their eventual decisions—for all of them it had taken time—had been life-changing responses to experience, arising from healing, answered prayer, community engagement, visions, or spiritual awakenings. Even years later they were still digesting and awed by these experiences, and so willing to accommodate my own exploration of what God was doing with me.

An interfaith colleague suggested I needed to relate to the serious arguments of those who opposed MRP and referred specifically to Daniel Strange, who held that non-Christian religions were "human idolatrous responses to divine revelation behind which stand deceiving demonic forces".[75] This might have been expected to lead to advice that Christians should not engage with other religions, but Strange called on Evangelicals to immerse themselves in the lives of the religious other, recognizing the power of God's grace to subversively fulfil the other religion by correcting the distortions of divine truth it has introduced. My position is that it is only when one attempts such immersion that one finds out how Christian grace operates in that situation, while recognizing that subversive fulfilment is one possible outcome. A sign of the difference between our approaches was found among his examples of this subversive fulfilment, where the contrast was drawn between the determinist views of other faiths and the interpersonal dialogue of Christian calling. I believe this stereotype oversimplifies both Christian and other-religion views to the point of error. Ephesians 1:3–14: "he chose us in Christ before the foundation of the world . . . He destined us for adoption . . . he has made known to us the mystery of his will . . . a plan for the fullness of time" sounds pretty determinist, whereas the regular Sikh reading of the *hukamnama*, the randomly chosen passage of scripture that offers direction for each day, is clearly understood as a dialogical practice through which God speaks directly to an individual or community and invites a lived response. More fundamentally Strange's determinism/dialogue polarity is the sort of distinction, similar to determinism/free will, where an understanding of the work of an omniscient creator who is also a liberator opens up a paradox—or an aspect of cognitive dissonance—rather than a blunt alternative. Another sign of our different approaches was that although Strange briefly described his Christian-Hindu family background, he gave no indication of how his theoretical position related to that background, nor was there any other indication of how the complexities of lived experience relate to the doctrinal absolutes described.[76]

Fairly early on I had requested a discussion about my research with some neighbouring Anglican clergy, and was surprised to find that even the request provoked a lively correspondence as to whether it was appropriate to discuss such challenging behaviour at all. It was eventually decided to proceed, and the meeting turned out to be friendly and attentive, with a conversation that was sometimes supportive, and sometimes neutrally questioning. There was just one barbed question: "Does the Bishop know you are doing this?" to which the answer was "yes"; but there was also anxiety:

> I struggle that a Christian minister could in any way participate in the worship of another faith without undermining their loyalty to Christ. I understand your reasons for wanting to enter their world, but I struggle because of what Christ means to you, and the impact of it on you spiritually. My concern is a pastoral one for your safety spiritually...

This followed an example of spiritual danger from engaging with the occult which had parallels with Strange's position. I did not have an answer as to how the experience might affect my relationship with Jesus, as that was one of the things I was hoping to find out, but I referred to the constant need for discernment in interreligious, Christian, and secular settings alike. Throughout my research this was the meeting at which I was most clearly challenged, but it was done in friendship. It sharpened my awareness that there were issues of loyalty and betrayal that I had not fully worked out and it no doubt played its part in my picking up Margalit's book described above. I also had a notably supportive message afterwards:

> I think it is really great, John, that you are engaging so intensively with such wonderfully spiritual people and just wanted to express my encouragement and approval for . . . your commitment to genuine experimental interfaith dialogue. God bless you . . . and I pray that your work and witness will be of value to all of us . . .

Reflections on a family crisis

Much more personally significant than these ecclesial challenges was a crisis that came on our family in August 2016. My daughter and her husband Peter[77] had just announced they were expecting their first child when Peter, who had been finding walking increasingly difficult, was diagnosed as having a tumour that was damaging his spinal cord. Surgery was risky, but without it there was the likelihood of extensive paralysis, even death. Suddenly the need to pray was urgent.

I had just interviewed a convert from *Sikhi* to Christianity who had experienced a number of healings, some at a large evangelical and charismatic church near Birmingham. This church has midweek prayers for healing, and I attended them for the three weeks leading up to Peter's surgery. One of his work colleagues was a regular attender and had, unknown to me, brought him a prayed-over handkerchief from there as a blessing, a coincidence that, when I was told about it, helped me feel I had been right to be there. I appreciate charismatic Christians for their awareness of experience as important to faith, but my engagement with these meetings was also a time of submission. The hundreds of people there felt like a reprimand to my ministry to small congregations, and the preaching included condemnation of same-sex relationships and scathing comments on multiculturalism, both of which grated with me. The prayers for healing involved standing at the front of church with scores of others while a general prayer was said, giving me the Naaman-like thought, "Is this it?"[78] I participated as much as I could, now driven not by the excitement of exploration but by urgent need. Janice and I also asked for prayer at church, and we prayed together at home. I was so chastened by the experience that I did not ask for prayer at the gurdwara at first in case I offended the Christian God. When I did eventually ask the response was immediate and heartfelt; a Punjabi prayer was crafted and offered and regular enquiries about Peter's health followed, continuing throughout the fieldwork. I was advised at the gurdwara to pray to Jesus as well as praying there, and reflected on how unlikely it was that any Christian would give parallel advice to someone from a Sikh background.

Peter's operation was successful. The rediscovered harmony of Christian and Sikh prayer after the tearing apart of my first response seemed to mirror the healing the family shared in as Peter gradually recovered.

This experience related to my research. First, confidence in the rightness of my MRP, apparently secure when tested by colleagues, melted away when faced with a personal crisis; I had clung to my Christian roots and instinctively turned away from *Sikhi*. Second, there was a difference between my espoused theology—that which I told myself I believed—and my operative theology—that which I had been acting out. My espoused understanding was of God as gentle and kind, exercising a chosen vulnerability which is nonetheless universally significant, a self-emptying arising from humble divine choice. In contrast my operative theology had been revealed as that of a powerful God willing and able to command the smallest details of life—the tumour was the size of a blueberry—but also capricious and vengeful, who might be teaching me a lesson and need assuaging. It revealed that I was not just dealing with a contrast between two internal theological positions, liberal Christianity and *Sikhi*, but at least one other with this interventionist God, and possibly legion, only to be revealed as circumstances changed. Was this what I really believed underneath the sophisticated gloss I was presenting? But must I accept my thraldom to a view of God—and life—that was activated under such stress? This question seems unanswerable, but my response was not so much one of conservative Christianity, more the animism (some might say superstition) Stringer presents as the elementary form of English religious life.[79] It recalled Stephen Pattison's description of spirituality as "the experience and process of engaging with and managing significant relations and attachments", a wide and raw thing of which religion is only one aspect.[80] I experienced the frailty of my individual religious identity, but I must add that both religious communities proved deeply supportive. There was none of the conflict between religious demands that has so upset some mixed-faith families faced with sickness or bereavement.

There was a sad postscript to my story when Peter's devout young colleague suddenly and unexpectedly died some months later. Had God somehow taken her life as a love offering in return for Peter's health and the wellbeing of his family? That is neither a Christian nor a Sikh view, but rather another example of a more instinctive religious response to events.

Focal points

1. This research had a collaborative element. The author was the point of intersection of two involved communities. Seeking their permission was not a formality.
2. Large gaps in my understanding were being exposed despite my being an experienced interfaith officer who had known the gurdwara for some time. This was a new way of learning.
3. Being Christian was not my only significant identity. I was made aware of my white-Britishness, cultural difference from the community, and my role as researcher. Negotiating those was to be a significant aspect of my research.
4. I had pitched my degree of engagement at a modest level that was compatible with my ministry and would be for other DIFAs. Even that caused some disturbance of domestic and church arrangements.
5. Wearing the turban raised the question of play-acting with regard to the whole project, an anxiety not resolved quickly. There was also an element of playful enjoyment for myself and for some Sikh friends.
6. I had not appreciated the issue over changing my communion practice, and there were other issues I would be slow to attend to, showing the value of guided reflection.

7. Loyalty to the gurdwara developed over a period of a few months, driven by friendship and habit.
8. MRP is regarded by some as bringing with it the threat of spiritual danger. One of the roles of this research must be to describe the experience and its fruits with sufficient integrity to allow the reader (and writer) to exercise discernment over this.
9. I revealed under stress a very different frame of religious interpretation to that I espoused. Latent religious identities can be revealed or generated by changing circumstances. I was not dealing with a simple Christian/Sikh internal dialogue.

5
Community identities

As my place in the gurdwara as guest and student became settled and as I carried on through the various challenges that arose, it seemed time to explore the wider Sikh context with which I was engaging, something I had deliberately left for a while so that my initial experience at the gurdwara would not be shaped in advance by in-depth reading. I had skin in the game as I investigated religious and other aspects of the complex nature of Sikh identity and tried to find out how much I might, in time, be able to fit in. This was an emotional as well as theoretical exploration.

Sikhi as a faith identity

Guru Nanak only referred to *Sikhi* once, where a "Sikh" is taken to mean one having instruction, guided by teaching, a student, leading Devsi and others to say that I was already a Sikh in that regard. However, "Who is a Sikh?" is not just a religious issue but also concerns a secular ethical tradition, ethnic identity, issues of caste and of sects, complex relationships with Hindus and Muslims, imperialist meddling, orientalist distortions, a bloodstained engagement with the Indian state, a homeland that spreads across the Indo-Pakistan border, and the complexities of the diaspora.

Three institutions offer the illusion of order: the *Khalsa*, the *Akal Takht*, and the *Rehat Maryada*. The *Khalsa* is composed of those men and women who have undergone *amrit*, in which Sikhs commit themselves to the Five Ks: *kesh*, uncut hair, *kara*, a steel bracelet, *kanga*, a wooden comb, *kaccha*—or *kachh* or *kachera*—cotton underwear, and *kirpan*, a sword or dagger. They make commitments to eschewing alcohol and to regular prayer, including daily prayer before dawn. Other Sikhs may adopt some of these or wear them on occasion, but many turban-wearing and otherwise observant Sikhs leave this stage until old age or never enter it at all; Devsi was seventeen years in preparation. *Amritdhari* Sikhs are sometimes presented as typical, but are a minority. GKN has around the overall national figure of 10 per cent, respected but with no specific role in the management of the gurdwara.[81] The *Khalsa's* demands have resulted in the recognized category of *patit*, the lapsed, and in punishable breaches of discipline, *tankah*. However *Amritdhari* should not be regarded as the elite of *Sikhi*, there is no conversion rite to becoming a Sikh, and the main characteristic of *Sikhi* is following *bani*, Sikh teachings leading to harmony with other people arising from union with the divine, including non-discrimination, tolerance, hard work, sharing income, and spending time with needy people.[82]

The *Akal Takht*, the judicial authority at the *Harmander Sahib*, the Golden Temple, represents the authority of five leading gurdwaras over worldwide *Sikhi*, though the standing of the head of the court, its *Jathedar*, has been a matter of dispute, as has the role of the *Shiromani Gurdwara Parbandhak* Committee, the SGPC, which makes the appointments. The *Akal Takht* issues practical instructions of sometimes surprising detail, such as an edict saying no more gurdwaras are to be built in Wolverhampton and the money spent instead on education and healthcare.

The *Rehat* (or *Reht*) *Maryada*, a rulebook for the *Khalsa*, which dates from 1945, includes a definition of who is a Sikh. This goes beyond *Amritdhari*, but has belief in the significance of *amrit* as a required characteristic. It also forbids Sikhs to owe allegiance to any other religion. The importance of this to my own quest is clear, but the standing of the *Rehat Maryada* is greater in theory than practice. Despite a Sikh upbringing, Opinderjit Takhar first came across it as an undergraduate, and reckons most diaspora-born Sikhs are unaware of it; and a visitor to a large and well-organized gurdwara told me a copy could not be found on the premises. When its authority is cited, e.g. over mixed marriages, Sikh opponents of its more conservative stance feel free to dismiss it. Beside the *Amritdhari*, the *Rehat Maryada* also recognizes *Sahajdhari* Sikhs, those who have not taken *amrit*. They are described as "slow adopters", a description which idealizes the *Khalsa* by seeing all Sikhs as aspiring towards it. *Sahajdhari* Sikhs are further grouped by some as *Keshdhari*, those with turbans and uncut hair, and *mona*, clean-shaven and without turbans, though this latter term can be considered abusive. Those who were early followers of Guru Nanak but not clearly distinguished from the wider Hindu culture around them were known as *Nanak panthi*, a term still used as an epithet for such sects as the *Nirankaris* who reject the *Khalsa* form. The issue I faced was to clarify whether any of these descriptions—clearly not *Amritdhari*—could be appropriate for me.

Like all major religions, *Sikhi* has been formed in relation to others, a relationship in continuous flux. Hew McLeod, a New Zealander and for many years the leading Western academic in the area of Sikh studies, proposed that the original loose identification of *Nanak panthi* as followers of the Guru within wider Hindu society was overlaid by the establishment of the *Khalsa* in 1699, which he characterized as having a martial approach associated with the *Jat* social grouping (though they were traditionally farmers), and then by the religious labelling associated with the law and administration of the British Raj.[83] Harjot Oberoi responded to this, using Sikh historical materials to show that complex religious identities, including what would now be thought of as MRP, were commonplace within *Sikhi* long after the establishment of the *Khalsa*. He claimed that new communication methods and internal Sikh politics at the end of the nineteenth century, notably the rise of the *Tat Khalsa* reform movement, were the deciding factors in establishing a clear Sikh identity, rather than *Jat* or colonialist influence. This already existing identity was then codified by the British administration, political and military, and was strengthened by confrontations with Christian missionaries and reformed Hinduism.[84] However, this presentation of *Sikhi* as a late construct has itself been widely rejected, with claims that since the time of the second Guru (1539–52) Sikhs were a distinct community for which Guru Nanak had himself put down the markers.[85] That claim of distinctiveness from the start is important to many Sikhs, although a number of turbaned Sikhs do attend Wolverhampton *mandir* (Hindu temple) for Diwali, and I have seen attenders at GKN gurdwara wearing the Hindu thread, *jenoi*, alongside their *kara*. Some Punjabi Sikhs may engage in Hindu practices or other folk-religious activity, but the distinctiveness that contrasts with this has consequences for anyone wishing to engage with *Sikhi* in MRP: Bhai Gurdas (1551–1636), the first *Jathedar* of *Akal That*, compared a person who has multiple religious alliances with a prostitute, promiscuous and undiscerning.

As to the contacts between *Sikhi* and Christianity, the first to be recorded was a meeting in 1581 between Bhai Gurdas and some Jesuits, who he dismissed as "self-centred and confused".[86] Most contacts are much more recent.[87] John Parry, whose studies arose out of his own missionary work, traced the Christian mission in the Punjab back to 1833 and noted that reaction to this missionary effort had led to the formation of a second reform movement, *Singh Sabha*, intended to improve Sikh education and protect a sense of Sikh identity. Relations between Sikhs and Christians could be positive and respectful, exemplified by C. H. Loehlin, a Presbyterian missionary who was so well respected he was invited to speak at *Harmander Sahib*, the Golden Temple, and by Gopal Singh, the Sikh who wrote *The Man Who Never Died*, a devotional poem about Jesus Christ. In contrast relationships could be confrontational and dismissive, as with the abusive Christian missionary Ernest Trumpp, or the Sikh tract-writer Bhai Vir Singh. There were also those such as Pandit Waljit Bhai and Tahil Singh who refused to regard the two religions as "other" to each other at all, but that peaceable approach did not survive the contest that was developing.[88] The missionaries' change of focus in favour of the *dalits*, and then the souring of mood following the attack on *Harmander Sahib* in 1984, halted dialogue and in India it has never recovered.[89]

In the UK, Parry was engaged in a United Reformed Church Sikh/Christian consultation which had been inaugurated in 1984,[90] and in 1993 Owen Cole and Piara Singh Sambhi wrote *Sikhism and Christianity: A Comparative Study*, which discussed the nature of grace and of incarnation and the meaning of "kingdom". Latterly engagement has been intermittent, although in 2019 a Sikh-Christian Forum was launched at Wolverhampton University and has met at different locations in the West Midlands since.[91] Ruth Lambert has investigated what Christians can learn from their encounter with Sikhs, and some scriptural reasoning now includes consideration of the *Guru Granth Sahib Ji* beside the Bible and the Qur'an.[92]

The ambivalence in the relationship between Sikhs and Christians was exemplified at GKN at Christmas 2016, when the Punjabi newspaper distributed there, *Mann Jitt Weekly*, included several Christmas greetings with illustrations of the Sacred Heart, some alongside pictures of the martyrdom of Guru Gobind Singh's sons which is marked at that time. In contrast to those signs of togetherness was a pile of pamphlets warning Sikhs not to get involved in Christmas celebrations as they were satanic.[93] No-one at the gurdwara knew who had put them there, but they demonstrated a defensiveness also found on the internet in the face of Christianity. Sikhs dislike the idea of conversion, remembering bloody forced conversions by Muslims and the ties of Christian missions with imperialism, and *Sikhi's* universalism sees changing religion as lacking ultimate significance and resisting *karma*, the destiny established by actions in previous lives. This was problematic for some in relating to my project. "We do not seek converts" was not far from implied criticism of my attempt to flex religious identity. In turn, I am uneasy about the rejection of conversion, the opportunity for which is from my perspective an aspect of religious freedom.

I have a concern for interfaith relations generally, so how *Sikhi* relates to faiths other than Christianity is important to me. Pashaura Singh acknowledges the tension between the drive to establish and defend Sikh identity and a tradition of religious accommodation, but he draws insight from the presence within *Guru Granth Sahib Ji*, the heart of Sikh identity, of the compositions of Hindu and Muslim saints, a presence which points to the possibility that the "other" might somehow become oneself. He also points out that in the *pangat*, the sitting together without distinction at the meal which is an integral part of Sikh worship, the divide between Sikh and non-Sikh is deliberately obliterated along with those between nationalities and castes.[94]

When I started attending GKN, one of the musicians was a Muslim, and this was a matter of satisfaction as his presence recalled Mardana, Guru Nanak's Muslim musician and companion. There were regular reminders that religions should not divide people following Guru Nanak's founding declaration "there is no Hindu, there is no Muslim", and the wider Vedic philosophy that religion is a matter of birth, of *karma*, rather than conversion. However, tensions with Muslims, historic and current, recurred in conversation. My reaction is complex; for example, I am unsure about the regular accusations of Muslim attempts to convert Sikh women. Research has not substantiated it, and so I am neither willing to take it into my worldview nor am I in a position to challenge it.[95] I had to ask whether identifying with *Sikhi* entails taking on some of the wariness, self-justifications and hostilities that have arisen from their history. This must be a matter of degree for me as it is for established Sikhs who in conversation place themselves at very different places on this spectrum of suspicion.

An appealing aspect of *Sikhi's* view of other religions is its tradition of secular government and defence of religious freedom. Guru Teg Bahadur (1621–75) suffered torture and martyrdom to prevent Hindus being forcibly converted to Islam, and this tolerance was present in the Sikh empire established in the eighteenth century, which had Persians, Hindus, and a (presumably Christian) Frenchman in the government. Sikhs have sometimes been caught up in communal violence but there is no record of attempts at forced conversion, something of which Sikhs can be justly proud, and which shows up a contrasting Christian history. The Sikh secular tradition offers a principled separation of religion and state that in its libertarian fundamentals is impressive, and, to a member of an established church, challenging.

Sikhi as a nationality

Guru Nanak had followers in many parts of India and beyond, and the original *Khalsa*, the *Panji Pyari*, came from all over the Indian subcontinent. However, largely in the face of the Mughal threat, there developed a number of states with Sikh rulers, including Ranjit Singh's empire (1799–1839). Sikhs particularly identify with the Punjab, an area much greater than the modern state, which was split at partition between Pakistan and India. The violent response of the Indian government to Punjabi separatism, in particular the assault on *Harmander Sahib* in 1984 and the massacre of Sikhs across India following Indira Gandhi's murder, focussed this nationalist feeling. Among Sikh nationalists struggling for their own land of Khalistan, "the Country of the Pure", recent evidence of

British complicity in the attack on *Harmander Sahib* has caused renewed resentment. The Jallianwala Bagh massacre at the hands of the British in 1919 also came to the forefront recently through the British prime minister's failure to formally apologize during his 2013 visit and his successor's expression of regret in 2019.

Nationalist and religious zeal can run together: the flashpoint for the 1970s unrest in Punjab arose out of a sectarian dispute, a religious spark to a political movement. They can also contradict each other. Takhar's suggestion that sectarian differences be subsumed in a wider Sikh federation provoked hostility from religious purists, although it would create a stronger political front. Sikhs living in the West have their own issues, such as turban-wearing and *kirpan*-carrying, a reminder that the political identity of *Sikhi* does not just concern nationalist issues.

GKN is less nationalistic than many gurdwaras, shown by people's willingness to identify as Indian. When an MP told them that he was opposing the extradition to India of Parmjit Singh Saini, accused of being a Sikh terrorist, some feeling was expressed in favour of extradition and the MP's efforts were not universally appreciated. I attended a national *Ramgarhia* Association meeting where the Indian vice-consul was a key speaker, and those there listened attentively to an appeal for the 1.5 million people of Indian extraction in the UK to work together rather than in separate communities. This can be contrasted with the claim that 225 out of 270 British gurdwaras have banned Indian officials from their premises on political grounds.[96]

The injustices Sikhs have faced and the political aspirations of some aroused my sympathies as I got to know about them, but they did not feel like my battles. I wanted to develop in the religious aspects of *Sikhi*, but less so the political. Whenever Indian political issues were being considered I was conscious of my post-imperial cultural situation, brought up with a positive view of empire now being painfully unlearned, and in quiet conversation the effects of British meddling, particularly the devastating consequences of partition, were brought home to me. There are sharp questions about national identity in engaging with *Sikhi* from a white British background.

Sikhi as an ethnicity

Many Sikhs regard *Sikhi* as an ethnicity as well as a religion. The Sikh Federation UK views the current option in the UK census of recording Sikhism as a religion as inadequate, and has run a campaign over many years to have a box allowing Sikhs to identify themselves as ethnically Sikh, something they can currently do only by themselves writing "Sikh" against the ethnicity question. Recognizing *Sikhi* as an ethnicity would be in accordance with a House of Lords ruling in 1983, *Mandla vs Dowell Lee*, which found that Sikhs are an ethnic group for the purposes of the Race Relations Act 1976. The court made the point that "ethnic" in this context is not to be identified with "racial", leaving open the possibility of a white British person being ethnically Sikh.

The suspicion of conversion identified above can reinforce the ethnic aspect of *Sikhi*, though white converts I interviewed seemed unaware of this, one having been well received by a university Sikh society, another having been invited at yoga class to hear a Sikh speaker, and a third having been engaged by a street mission from *Basics of Sikhi*. I met such an evangelist at a feeding station, witnessing a half-hour discussion between him and a couple of clients. On the *Basics of Sikhi* website there are testimonials from Christian and other white British and Canadian converts, and descriptions of regular street missions, *parchar*. At present white converts who join in Punjabi congregations still attract attention. One convert commented: "A lot of times what does happen is that we are used as an example because we are atypical. Most white Sikhs typically have come into Sikhism through Yogi Bhajan [3HO], and they are branded in a certain way, and that's not our focal point, we are just mainstream."

The Sikh Dharma[97] *of the Western Hemisphere*, also known as 3HO, "Healthy, Happy, Holy Organization", is particularly associated with white, *gora*, converts. Despite—or perhaps because of—being more zealous than many Punjabi Sikhs, they are regarded with a suspicion that is not allayed by their claiming the authority of the *Akal Takht* for a leadership role among Sikhs in the West. Disputed issues include the 3HO practices of yoga, ordaining ministers, and allowing women among the ceremonial *panj pyare*, representing the five beloved ones who founded the *Khalsa*.

A Punjabi woman interviewee told me this latter is seen as a category mistake to which non-Punjabis are liable rather than as a feminist move. Furthermore the organization's founder, Yogi Bhajan, who died in 2004, has in recent years faced persistent accusations of sexual abuse.

All religion is encultured, and Punjabi *Sikhi* is infused with a sense of *izzat*, family honour, in many aspects of everyday behaviour, something which *gora* Sikhs are regarded as incapable of appreciating or accommodating properly. The issue of language also features in this cultural divide; Punjabi Sikhs are aware that *gora* Sikhs find it difficult to speak or understand Punjabi, and this limits the amount to which they can truly be accepted in the community.

Not surprisingly, marriage has the potential to point up these issues. I spoke with one white couple who had a Sikh religious wedding, *anand karaj*, but they were both already *Amritdhari*. Neither of the white married partners of Punjabis I interviewed had a wedding in that form, and doing so would provoke hostility among some Sikhs, even violent intervention from a small minority. I was told of a couple where the bride was white and she and her Punjabi groom had to go—along with many guests including my informant—to Italy for a gurdwara wedding, impossible in their own countries, England and Holland. The bride had taken part in the Sikh and Punjabi preliminaries, so I asked whether the problem was her ethnicity or her religion. He asked around the family and told me no-one knew; without the clear commitment of *amrit* the status of non-Punjabis engaging with *Sikhi* remains unclear, even to family members. White people I spoke to who had married Punjabis felt welcome in their gurdwaras and Sikh communities despite not having had *anand karaj*, though one described the painstaking steps needed to win over the family. One Punjabi Sikh who had married a white woman from a Christian background told me that their (secular) marriage had not caused an issue, but that the question of Sikh identity and his desire to attend the gurdwara had grown since the birth of their son, something they were working out between them.

Sikhs welcome visitors, but my wish to worship as a Sikh was challenging for my hosts, and this was influenced by ethnic factors. I saw few white people at GKN, and, except for those who had married Punjabis, they were clearly guests. However, the steady trickle of non-Punjabi converts, particularly in the USA, means that Sikhs are finding they have to distinguish between the religious and cultural aspects of their heritage. My participation was raising this issue for those around me.

Between *gora* Sikhs and Punjabis in the West there is the further issue of the racism Sikhs face. It was only after knowing him a long time that a Sikh friend told me what happened when, as a young man recently arrived in this country, he went to a celebration of New Year in Trafalgar Square. Without any warning, he was head-butted and left shocked and bleeding. Despite the crowds all around him only one person offered any sympathy, and the policeman he approached dismissed the incident, with the comment, "What do you expect me to do about it?" He fled, beginning the New Year injured, frightened, and alone. To hear these things was to feel diffidence in asking to be accepted by people who had suffered historically, recently, communally, and individually from my own ethnic and national group, but this diffidence was reduced by my apparent acceptance by those around me.

This reflection reminded me of the ethnic aspect of my inhabiting Christianity. Being white I rarely sense the low-key preference given to white cultural norms in my own background and in a church still being identified in 2020 as institutionally racist.[98]

Caste and class

Caste should not have affected my belonging to *Sikhi*, which rejects caste discrimination, demonstrated by *langar* being a shared meal across caste, *panj pyare* being drawn from different castes, *amrit* being from a shared bowl, and *seva* thrusting people into defiling roles like shoe-cleaning. Caste may not be thought to concern me, as I was told there is no direct attempt to place white British in the caste system, though marriage to a white person can be a challenge to a family's honour. However, there remains a consciousness of caste within Punjabi culture as a preference for one's own kind in family affairs, as an aspect of *izzat*, and as discrimination. On a visit to a *Ravidassi* temple[99]

there was an explosion of pain when it was explained that the
temple had started [separated from the gurdwara] when a lower
caste person whose son had died tried to have a prayer said in
the gurdwara. It wasn't allowed.

Takhar considered the issue of Sikh identity through the nature of its sects and for some groups, notably the *Ravidassis* and the *Valmikis*, the point of focus is caste.[100] "Caste" is taken by some to refer only to the classic Hindu schema of *Brahmins, Kshatriyas, Vaishyas*, and *Shudras*. Here what is being referred to is *zat*, that is, inherited occupational groupings. Kiyotaka Sato demonstrated clear caste delineations in a study of the characteristics of Leicester gurdwaras, and there is a similar situation in Wolverhampton.[101]

GKN is a *Ramgarhia* gurdwara, and I was told that *Ramgarhia* means "Custodians of the Castle of God", not a caste but a *misl*, descendants of a military unit formed for the defence of *Harmander Sahib*, a unit which became for a while the ruling group in the Sikh kingdom. However, there remains awareness of the occupational grouping from which the *Ramgarhia* were drawn, the carpenters of the *Tarkhan* and blacksmiths of the *Lohar* groupings, which have some of the social dynamic associated with caste. The extended family aspect was exemplified for me at the national *Ramgarhia* Association meeting when there was much excited chatter as families from many different areas of Britain gathered together. *Ramgarhia* have suffered from caste discrimination, and an experienced DIFA told me that he finds among them a sense of equality, an egalitarian movement, far more than in other Sikh communities. I was told that GKN's predecessor was set up because the other gurdwaras in Wolverhampton were dominated by *Jats* and would never appoint *Ramgarhia* people to their committees, and I came across a Sikh problem page online where a *Jat* asked whether she could be justified in marrying a *Ramgarhia* boyfriend. One reply quoted the Sikh rejection of caste, but another warned against upsetting parents and the wider family by pursuing the relationship. When I told *Jat* friends that I was attending a *Ramgarhia* gurdwara, they dismissed the need for caste-based gurdwaras at first, but then acknowledged that no *Ramgarhia* would ever be elected to their gurdwara committee, though no-one would ever say so publicly.

I could clearly never be admitted to the *misl*, but my sympathies were engaged with them as victims of discrimination, by discovering their glorious but under-acknowledged history, and on being invited to attend their joyful national gathering.

I was gradually learning the limitations of my belonging, but it took time for me to wonder how the management committee, the central body of the gurdwara, was appointed and by whom. It was elected by the members, so I enquired about becoming a member; one of the few occasions in my fieldwork where as a researcher I went beyond what I might have done naturally, prompted by Stobert's encouragement to push the boundaries. A trustee gave me a copy of the constitution and discussed it with me. The official title of the organization was the "Ramgarhia Board (Sikh Temple) Wolverhampton", and it made clear that membership was only open to members of the *Ramgarhia* community.

I had come up against a model of religious membership with which I was unfamiliar. The courtesy of my hosts had held them back from raising an aspect of gurdwara life in which I could not participate, and there was in any case some diffidence about the *misl*-based nature of the gurdwara, as advice had been given that this could be a source of legal trouble for them. I was touched that Devsi took it upon himself to pursue with the president the idea of an associate membership for me as a regular attender not from a *Ramgarhia* background. The president replied that it was an interesting idea and that he would ask what committee members thought, which I took to be a polite rejection. Despite Devsi asking again nothing came of it, but later there were developments over caste in the gurdwara which were to directly involve me.

This consideration of caste made me think about class issues in church. I was in a minority, perhaps alone at Beacon Church, in having been privately educated, and had been brought up in a wealthier suburb a few miles away, but this did not seem very distinctive from the home-owning families sending their children off to university all around us. It also accorded with the outdated expectation that Anglican clergy are going to be middle-class which may still be there in older church members. I was not conscious of class in that setting as a rule, but now wondered if others were, and, if so, in what way. A rule of research like this is not to include material that may be painfully over-revealing and that comes to mind as I make these comments on my class, particularly stating that I was privately educated and so, in a British culture, inevitably placing myself under the judgement of the reader. If it is hard for someone from another cultural background than the Indian subcontinent to find an open guide to caste issues, I must also recognize a corresponding awkwardness for white British people about class, despite research clearly showing how all-pervasive it is, and how much it affects our lives.

Sexuality and gender

Some aspects of my outward identity affected the mode rather than the degree of my belonging. I was presenting as straight, and so did not have to negotiate negative perceptions of gay identity. Although these issues are not formalized in *Guru Granth Sahib Ji* or in Sikh rules of lifestyle, and some Sikhs take a liberal attitude, many Sikhs agree with wider Indian culture in regarding gay orientations negatively.[102] This is not to say my straight approach was all gain as a gay standpoint could alter a researcher's perspective to advantage. James Alison described his framework of perception as a gay Catholic as exploring "the shape of a new story that starts to emerge where there is a rupture in impossibility", and Michelle Voss Roberts identified a specific parallel between gay experience and MRB.[103]

A woman researcher would have had a very different pattern of access. Men and women sit separately in the *durbar* and tend to separate in the *langar* hall, and women have their own midweek meeting. I remember a discussion between men about gurdwara affairs when a nearby woman muttered "bloody politics!", hinting at a perspective on this male-dominated community about which a woman researcher would have discovered much more. A specifically feminist approach would also have led to quite different questions and structural approaches to belonging, although I recognize that the gender of the researcher need not control whether such an approach is used.[104] I had to recall that this was not an ethnographic study of the gurdwara itself, but an account of my own participation, with all the specificity that entailed.

I was appreciatively aware that a tradition of gender equality in *Sikhi* goes back to Guru Nanak, standing out in Indian history and centuries ahead of Western culture, and came to know of powerful women like Mai Bhago and other wives who led their deserter husbands back to a battle against terrible odds at Khidrana, and whose leadership is widely celebrated in the *sangat*.[105] A woman, Bibi Jagbir Kaur, has twice been elected president of the SGPC; and Princess Sophia Duleep Singh was a notable figure in the British suffragette movement. Sikh women are recognized as including many high achieving professionals.[106] However, domestic abuse is present among Sikhs as in all communities, sometimes exacerbated by the tensions of *izzat*, and it was good to see it being acknowledged one Sunday by a presentation in the gurdwara from a city-wide organization called *Say "No" to Violence Against Women and Girls*.[107] Orange ribbons were handed out to signify support and were widely worn by women and men. However, some patriarchal attitudes linger. Women were only allowed to serve on GKN's committee after the threat of appeals to anti-discrimination tribunals and to the *Akal Takht*. I was not aware of women being on the committee while I was there, nor is it usual elsewhere, though women have taken the lead in British gurdwaras in the event of male leadership proving unsustainably chaotic.[108] In the GKN gurdwara, the washing up, in theory an opportunity for anyone to offer *seva*, is largely done by women. Men help serve food but rarely prepare it.

Other reflections on gender are more personal, a reminder that mine is a "male gaze":[109]

> I noticed a young woman with a dress the colour of sunlight stood close to the front. Straight away she turned round as though knowing someone was looking at her. I hastily looked away, so don't know whether she looked in my direction or not, but felt embarrassed, caught out.

I seldom approached any younger women and noted that they did not approach me or get introduced to me. The two exceptions were a white wife of a Punjabi who I approached about interviewing her and her husband, who was present but talking with someone else, but from whom

I never heard back; and the woman starting children's classes in Punjabi. When the classes did not emerge, I asked an older woman about it, and she said the prospective teacher would let me know. I had a message back saying it was not happening, but we never spoke directly. Older women, however, greeted me with as much friendship and kindness as the men:

> When I started washing up in the kitchen I was told I could get some flip-flops from outside, but before I could do so one of the women slipped her large slippers off and gave them to me. Nice and warm!

I contrasted my self-conscious experience as a male in the gurdwara with my failure to factor that into my understanding of the Church. My awareness of women's experiences in ministry developed as I trained two women curates, but only more recently have I recognized my own experience of the Church is not to be taken as standard, but is itself gendered, "malestream" rather than mainstream.[110] Lay leadership by women has increased, as much through the numerical majority of women over men as through any ideological change, but I remain insufficiently alert to stereotyping of roles.[111] Men helped with food preparation or washing up no more in Beacon Church than in the gurdwara.

What makes someone a Christian?

Considering Sikh identity was making me think about identity itself more carefully, and the specific question, "Who is a Christian?" This is in a context of people's multiple identities across different criteria, not just religion, nationality, and language, but regionality, political and social attitudes, and a host of other markers, many of them cutting across each other. Despite this complexity there is still a role for communities as well as individuals in the establishment of such identities. The community sets out what is allowed and even what is imaginable. My own move, though outside the normal range of either Christianity or *Sikhi*, has been made possible by a wider culture of freedom of religion, and respect for the possibility of choosing one's identity in other areas such as sexuality and gender. On the other hand individuals shape culture, and I had been aware of Christians and Sikhs alike reacting to my project, and in some cases rethinking their own attitudes. Within this wider context mixed religious identity is just one aspect, whether understood negatively as syncretism or religious consumerism, or arising naturally from mixed families or communities. There is also a fluidity of religious identity over time; people and communities change perhaps through specific experiences, as with some of the converts I interviewed, or through wider cultural changes, as in the western European drift away from Christian religious engagement.

Identity is questioned less in Christianity than in *Sikhi*, and there are some off-the-shelf answers to the question "who is a Christian?" These include liturgical tests related to baptism or participation in the Eucharist; doctrinal tests of faith in Jesus' death bringing salvation or in the Trinity; or experiential tests, being born again or speaking in tongues. My self-understanding as a Christian would be problematic in some quarters. There are groupings who regard Anglican or Methodist claims to be Christian as either defective or delusional, and others outside and within the Anglican Communion for whom liberal views over doctrine, sexuality, interreligious and interdenominational issues would be problematic. There are times every day when I would on reflection find my own actions or attitudes ethically "unchristian".

These judgements over Christian identity mostly operate in separate communal realms within which they seem self-evident, but after the Second Vatican Council (1962–65) there was a time when Catholic certainties were disturbed by the acknowledgement that some Protestants, while standing outside Roman Catholic structures and doctrinal authority, may still be Christians. Hans Küng and Hans Urs von Balthasar both addressed this issue, and from their contrasting viewpoints of social engagement on the one hand and aesthetic mysticism on the other came to similar conclusions. For Küng, Christians are called to adopt an attitude of absolute trust rather than chasing and relying on their own achievement. If we stop living for ourselves, we will gain meaning, identity, and freedom and become truly human.[112] For von Balthasar, a practising Christian is one who lives Christ's love, entering the personal humiliation of faith. The mark of believers is that they assent to God by making themselves available to him and to building the kingdom.[113]

There is a parallel with Vedic *karma* in this requirement to be available to God's will, so perhaps it is possible to fulfil the demands of two religions at once, a coherence through practice. However, the element of submission is not without its problems. At a focus group I was asked about my understanding of worship and referred to "two aspects: adoration and submission". A participant responded: "I feel happier with the adoration than the submission. I don't think I could be a Catholic or a Muslim because of the submission, that's not me." I replied that maybe "submission" was not quite the right word, and tried "letting go of ego" instead, to which participants responded "that's different", and I could only reply feebly, "I'm not sure it's as different as you think it is, but there we go." The exchange reminded me that "submission" has been so abused by the patriarchal Church as to be a suspect spiritual category. Submission is a particular problem in my own MRP. I am submitting to two people, Guru Nanak and Jesus, inevitably setting myself up as arbiter, a role that is incompatible with submission to either. And yet von Balthasar and Küng cannot be ignored in their call for submission; Christian and Sikh worship both have aspects of awed surrender. The typical Christian liturgy of any denomination includes a call to penitence and promise of moral and religious restoration, and *Guru Granth Sahib Ji*, a liturgical text as well as a scripture, requires *gurmukh*, walking in the way of the Guru by grace sought in prayer.

Raimon Panikkar offers a more fluid approach to Christian identity in the context of MRP, seeing it as having two aspects: the sincere confession of the individual; and the corresponding recognition of a community. It is a matter of relationship, and the way the individual or community makes those decisions can change over time. For Panikkar, this dynamic meaning-making points to a reality which is beyond both individual and community and to which they are being drawn.[114] As to my own confession and recognition, I had felt able to make a Christian confession throughout the research, and this self-identification was reciprocated by most Christians with whom I dealt.

The research also raised the issue of my belonging to the Beacon Church. I had written in a report to the church that "belonging" to the gurdwara was proving complicated and then added:

> As to church, as the minister I have a special place, but is it one of belonging? I am here for a limited time, parachuted in, and am greeted each week by the worship leader as though I am a visitor. On circuit (once a month) I come across fellowships and situations where I feel less at home than I now do in the gurdwara.

I discussed this with a Christian colleague, Deb Dyson:

> (Me:) "Church Council were a bit surprised that I'd raised the question, but a Methodist minister doesn't actually belong to a congregation but to the circuit, something I knew but had never really thought about."
>
> (Dyson:) "So that was something that has definitely come out of experiences at the gurdwara?"
>
> (Me:) "I don't think it would have occurred to me. And I'm not sure it's occurred to anyone in a theoretical sense. I'm sure it occurs to ministers the whole time on an emotional level, do I belong here or not? But I don't know of any theorizing at all."

Focal points

1. Whether I was a Sikh or a Christian was primarily a matter for the respective communities to decide, but I and other individuals can affect community judgements. These judgements occur at a meeting point between the institutional and historic and the personal and instinctive.
2. *Sikhi* has a clear identity of its own, but its history is interwoven with Hinduism, Islam and, recently, Christianity. These historic relationships bring opportunities and problems for friendly relations.

3. *Sikhi* is interwoven with *Punjabiat*, the cultural heritage and ethos of the people of the Punjab, and *gora* Sikhs are not entirely integrated into *Sikhi* as it stands, although this may change with time, place, and grouping. No religion exists in a "pure" state without cultural manifestation, and anyone seeking to participate in a religion has to negotiate that.
4. Different religions and different groupings within and across religions have markedly different ways of characterizing people and communities, including over the issue of belonging. Even formal membership is not always straightforward or universally available and discovering informal aspects of belonging can be a lengthy and testing process.
5. All the above (i–iv) are as true of Christianity as of any other religion, introducing an unexpected element of provisionality into my own Christian identity.
6. Issues of belonging need to navigate relationships with the idealized transnational faith community but also with the local congregation, *sangat* etc.
7. The individual's sexuality and gender exemplify those identity markers that affect both the place accorded them in the community and the lens through which they view their surroundings.

6

Becoming different

The sense that I had settled into the static role of welcome visitor was to prove illusory. There were challenges but there were also developments in my spiritual life and in my Sikh social context that were moving the relationship forward.

Praying at home

My limited aim was to find out how regular public worship with the *sangat* affected me, and so I did not commit myself to participate in Sikh life outside that, though I followed up any invitations which were practicable, like the national Ramgarhia Association meeting. I had two invitations to travel to India, one from the Canadian-based gurdwara and one from Devsi, but for practical reasons could not accept either. However, *Sikhi* did begin to make its mark on my prayers at home.

I have fallen back on some form of Morning Prayer—with many breaks—since my school days, and during the time of fieldwork was doing so when possible with a small group in a neighbouring parish. I also read through and became familiar with *Jap Ji*, the foundational Sikh scriptural passage, setting time aside, as well as referring to it on my phone when I had a few moments, until the gurdwara secretary said such casual reading was disrespectful. I set out to gradually read *Guru Granth Sahib Ji* through, something which Sikhs do over forty-eight hours at a special event in the gurdwara (*Akhand Paath*), but I got less than a third of the way. I knew the theory of the layout of *Guru Granth Sahib Ji*,[115] but could rarely find a piece from a reference given except by the standardized page numbers. I then switched to following the *hukamnama*, the chosen scripture, sometimes using the section displayed on the board at GKN, but more often the one issued at *Harmander Sahib* daily and widely available on apps and websites. For some months, I chose a few words from each passage, jotting them down with reflections.

Since 1987 I have engaged with the World Community for Christian Meditation (WCCM), sometimes using its mantra *maranatha*, "come Lord", in my own meditation. In Sikh meditation, *simran*, I used the refrain *Waheguru*, "wonderful Lord", a Sikh term for God. I experimented with using both together as their meanings did not clash, and they worked together rhythmically with similar stresses on the two words, but there remained something aesthetic rather than theological that jarred, so that, without realizing, I would revert to using one or the other alone. Perhaps introducing duality into this meditative setting was disruptive, or maybe the resulting phrase was over-complex. I continued to use both, but separately. They had exactly the same effect on me, including occasionally bursts of a delightful though ephemeral feeling of visual brightness, a floating, weightless sensation, and a physical joy with erotic parallels. When I heard a Western couple describing the union with God they had discovered in *simran*, I wondered whether it was something like these experiences to which they were referring: "You do *simran*, you get happiness" . . . "all of a sudden I had the bright light" . . . "you really do get experiences out of it that confirm you are on the right path."[116]

Sikh meditation is central to the practice of the faith, but it must be balanced by a practical side. The Sikh emblem, the *khanda*, displays two swords, *miri piri*, which recognize the military (*amir*) and spiritual (*pir*) aspects. The *khanda* is open to many interpretations including symbolizing the balanced practice of *Sikhi* in daily life and meditation.[117] Daily life includes *kirat karna*, providing for one's family by working for a living, which was originally a challenge to begging Hindu holy men and has also become part of the Sikh ethic of self-advancement. I have had a sustained employment history, but find myself wondering if I am still fulfilling this now I am retired. *Waand chhakna* is the sharing of one's earnings, something which I have practised by regular planned donations to Christian Aid. *Daswandh*, the donation of a tithe to the Guru, is mirrored to some extent by my donations to church. I also make contributions to the gurdwara when I attend, which seem on a par with the announcements of donations by others, though further substantial gifts must be made anonymously. These challenges of *Sikhi* are similar to those of Christianity, apart from the prudence of *kirat karna*, which has no clear parallel, and for me they bring the same mixed awareness of fulfilment and shortcoming.

Signs of friendship

The Beacon congregation was supportive of my engagement with *Sikhi*, and in June 2016, I asked if they would like to visit the gurdwara. Six said they would, though only three were eventually able to do so. We went one Saturday morning, a quiet time, which influenced their experience, and I was struck by their openness. It seemed to them a holy place where people were naturally prayerful, in contrast with the busyness they experienced at church, at which they all had responsibilities. They were impressed by the gentleness of the Sikhs they came across, the welcome they received, and the food which they contrasted favourably with the limited refreshments at church. They were interested in the development of the building, implying an expected strong future. In all they received a positive impression, which I did not attempt to shift although it is not always that peaceful there, and Sikhs are not so gentle when giving martial arts demonstrations. Their visit was affirmative of *Sikhi* and of my engagement with it. They also reported being drawn to pray there, without experiencing any challenge to their Christian identity.

This visit to the gurdwara was nearly matched by a Sikh outing to church, as I was asked to arrange a Christmas visit to the local church for a group. I prepared for a visit to Midnight Mass at a nearby church; the parish priest was most welcoming, and I told the gurdwara secretary what was going on as I did not wish it to be seen as undercover Christian evangelism. A couple of days before the visit, however, it became clear that no-one would be coming; the person who had approached me was unable to come herself and the others fell away.

My meditation in the gurdwara did not have the ecstatic aspect I occasionally experienced at home, but had developed a mellow warmth. It was as though the friendship I was experiencing round me was being matched, indeed surpassed, by what I was experiencing within. By December 2016, I had begun to reflect on this sensation: "Jesus says, 'I call you friends', and friendship with Guru Nanak, why not? His companions were friends too, and there need be no exclusivity in friendship." By February 2017, I was confirming that friendship (or friendliness as I more clearly defined the sensation) was to be a key theological theme. This linked back to my experience of Jesus' friendliness in the vision, to the friendship around me in gurdwara and church, and to stories of Nanak's own friendliness, as well as a sense of being drawn into a pre-existing friendship between Jesus and Nanak, similar to how some Christians experience the invitation of the Trinity.

Seva

My Sikh experience broadened following an interview with John Parry in which he linked Christianity and *Sikhi* through their shared emphasis on service to others. I was already doing *seva* by washing up at GKN, but that seemed a nominal engagement. I knew of feeding stations being run by Sikhs for people on the streets and contacted one of them, the Midland Langar Seva Society, becoming involved from March 2017 in serving hot food to homeless people every Monday evening in Birmingham, somewhere I would be able to continue to reach from my retirement address. I presented myself to those enquiring as someone trying to be a Sikh, not just an observer, as well as a Christian (I was then wearing my clerical collar) and recording the experience from my own point of view. The first sessions were in the pouring rain so I wore a coat with a hood, and with my grizzled appearance was indistinguishable from the clients, but after a week or two I began to be recognized as one of the team. The rain and cold and the obvious need of the people queueing ensured that this felt a real act of service. When it is dry, I wear the same headscarf as in the gurdwara, putting it on as I arrive as some of the other Sikhs do.[118] People mill about, expectant but anxious, waiting for a van to pull up with the orange Midland Langar Seva Society logo on it. Other helpers arrive by car, one bringing an urn of freshly cooked pasta. I twice helped cook this when I lived near the gurdwara where it was prepared, using the industrial-scale kitchen there:

> Before we begin, there is a time of prayer, and the Sikh standard is usually displayed. A normal meal consists of pasta, pizza, samosas, a drink, and a selection from fruit, crisps, biscuits or sweets, depending on what is available, and we feed around 160 people. I was invited to join in from the first time I went, often preparing the trays for the pasta. I work with perhaps half a dozen regular volunteers, Sikh families doing *seva* for some special occasion, and helpers who come from work as a part of their community involvement, so we are usually well staffed. Everyone is found something to do, recognizing the importance of *seva* for all participants. The volunteers treat the clients respectfully, some reserved and business-like, others friendly. The food is vegetarian, which the clients accept; this only becomes an issue when people come from a nearby Muslim feeding station and bring meat curry with them, when they are told to finish it before coming to us. I never see any communication between the feeding stations from the different religions.

Participation has introduced me to people, mainly younger, who take *Sikhi* seriously, attend a range of gurdwaras, and by their engagement offer an implied criticism to those whose *seva* is less demanding.

The employment tribunal

In March 2017, a committee member approached me as we moved out of the *durbar*: "Can I have a word with you afterwards please?" This felt a rather formal request, and I was uneasy as well as curious. "The committee would like you to write a letter to say that you have been allowed to do *seva*. It's for a tribunal." He explained the background, relating this request to a controversy that had been rumbling on in the gurdwara for some time. The Home Office allowed the *gurdwara* authorities to appoint *granthis* from India, appointments that led automatically to work permits (up to a set maximum number) being issued. The administration of these valuable appointments had led to bad feeling, even on one occasion to a few punches being swung and the police being called. The majority of the committee felt the permits had been wrongly handled and had tried to relieve the person dealing with this of his responsibility, something he had resisted, with some support from family members. His brother was now claiming that he had been prevented from standing for the committee on caste grounds and was taking a case for compensation to the tribunal. He said he had been prevented from doing *seva*, a prerequisite for election, because they thought he was not *Ramgarhia* (though in fact he was). The committee's response was that the post at issue was not a matter of employment, that the plaintiff hardly ever attended the gurdwara and that he had never offered *seva*, let alone been prevented from doing it. I was invited to write to say that, although not *Ramgarhia*, my *seva* of washing up had been welcomed.

This was something to be attested for their convenience but also felt like a sign of a new level of acceptance, and I wanted to please these committee members in return. On the other hand I was anxious about participating in such a wrangle, a principled worry about bullying, only having heard one side of the story, and a less principled one that by taking one side I would be making enemies on the other. I was warned that my letter would be passed on to the plaintiff's family and that I may hear from them, and family connections within the gurdwara meant I had no idea of the ramifications. I agreed to do it, sticking to the specific issue in hand. I heard nothing for several weeks, but then came a phone call asking me to write the letter that night and attend a tribunal the next day to swear to it as mine and face cross-examination. I handed it over that night, meeting a solitary trustee after dark outside the gurdwara gates like characters in a spy novel.

The next morning I attended the anonymous office block in Birmingham where the tribunal was to meet. Suddenly there was an influx of committee members, eight of them, arriving from Wolverhampton by train. They were suited, several were turbaned, and they were talking together, largely in Punjabi. They were very pleased to see me and seemed to take it in turns to keep me company. I was in my clerical collar and felt both my inclusion in and separateness from the group, and the ushers found it difficult to place me, rechecking more than once which case I was waiting for. When the gurdwara's barrister came, he did not pick up the issue about my *seva*, taking me instead as general evidence that non-*Ramgarhia* people were welcome in the gurdwara. The plaintiff failed to appear but was represented by a friend who had not been well briefed, and, despite the chair's help, was unable to show any employment issue was at stake. My letter was accepted without question, and I left for a parish appointment. My contribution seemed appreciated, but I was not convinced it had served much purpose. Later I had the message that the claim had failed, and the judge had also awarded the gurdwara costs, a major concern for them. Going into the gurdwara next Sunday I was greeted with appreciation by a number of members, leading others to ask what had been going on, giving me the unusual feeling of being an insider. The wider disagreement remains unsettled, however, and as late as February 2020 I was drawn aside by the plaintiff's friend to explain further developments from his point of view.

A sort-of ending

The specific time set aside for the research, the story-within-a-story, now come to a series of happy endings, but before sharing that happiness there is a need to acknowledge that my mistakes and confusion were a constant feature of the story.

After twelve months of research I presented a report to the GKN committee along with other interested parties, and I asked a friend to give it to the secretary at their next meeting. He looked confused and abashed, so I asked him what was wrong. There was a pause, then he said, "I *am* the secretary." Then who was the man who gave out the notices, who I was sure (or was I still?) people called "secretary"? My companion said, "Oh, he is the stage secretary, I am the committee secretary. If it's for the committee, would you like me to take it?" I was left wondering how I had gone so long without realizing there were two—or more—secretaries, and what else I was not understanding.

Coming up to the last month of my fieldwork, I had a bad day. "Wash your hands!" someone barked at me in the entrance hall. I had covered my head and taken off my shoes but had forgotten my ablutions. It was a disappointing sign, even after this time, of how little I was really enculturated, embodied, into gurdwara life. The gurdwara was crowded, with a large family programme going on. Things were ahead of the usual schedule, the *Ardas* had begun, so I did not make obeisance at the front but slunk in at the back. People were milling around, some on their mobiles, with plenty of noise coming from the *langar* hall. Behaviour may not have really been more casual than usual; perhaps, irritated after my rebuke, I noticed it more. It occurred to me that the familial nature of the *Ramgarhia* means that the people who come to such infrequent occasions are "us" in a way that I would never be, and that those who booked the programme would have made a substantial financial contribution to the gurdwara. My shame at my mean-spirited response to the large attendance, and my sense of marginality in the family gathering together with my earlier error over the handwashing, made this an uncomfortable day. Then on the way out someone commented on a recent terrorist attack: "Of course we've been fighting these people [Muslims] for 500 years. They are going to be doing this forever."

After two years of weekly attendance, my experience was still very different from that of cradle Sikhs around me. Devsi painted an idyllic picture of that family experience:

> Looking back I remember now my aunt, my father's cousin-sister, she told me stories, and I still remember them. An elderly person tells you stories, and you remember them all your life, which I am doing to my grandson as well. "Papa, two stories every night!" This is how you learn. You don't learn from books. You pass it on from generation to generation.

Realizing how little I know is humbling, but as such has the positive effect of challenging the *manmukh* (ego). I was an outsider and yet friendly corrections were beginning to build me into the community, meeting in partnership my attempts to identify with my hosts. People who had before probably only experienced guiding their own children were not just instructing me about the community but inducting me into it. It was sometimes said "as a student you need to know this" when I was corrected or given insights into the gurdwara management or politics, but it became apparent that they felt that I was on a longer term and more personal quest than just my academic studies. It is only after the fieldwork has finished that I can identify its continuing effect on me, but at the time I could indeed feel this community adoption working on my self-understanding. Apart from *amrit* there is no clear threshold of belonging in *Sikhi*, but the gossamer threads of instruction and friendship build surprisingly strong ties over time. Such mistakes may be evidence of learning, but I am conscious that readers, especially Sikhs, are likely to recognize errors of which I am still unaware, and the whole book therefore has a confessional and provisional element.

These awkward times did not take away from the occasions of celebration that marked the end of this period, the separate conclusions of my interfaith role, parish ministry, and Sikh fieldwork. It had long been my intention to retire from paid ministry after forty years, but I retired from the interfaith responsibilities several months earlier, when the opportunity came to pass the role to a particularly well-qualified candidate who had arrived in the diocese. We began, with the bishop's support, a handover that eventually took place in August 2016. A group of about forty people from across the area and across faiths gathered for my farewell, with food, an open microphone for speeches, a display of photographs, and a chance for people to write comments. I had a number of comments to treasure, including those from my bishop, who wrote of me as a "trustworthy guide" in the world of interfaith, referring to my "great energy, acumen and purpose", and my having endeared myself to all through my gentleness and humility, building up "huge reservoirs of trust and goodwill with all the faith communities as a result". I record these tributes as something of a balance to the description of my shortcomings, and to indicate the sharpness of the contrast between this appreciated role and that of student and initiate, pointing up the challenges the latter had involved.

Ending my interfaith role gave me more time in the parish, and this time was happy and fulfilling. On retirement the congregation generously invited people from my previous parishes to join them, arranging a Communion service and then a great tea party. The church was packed, every chair full and people sitting on the floor, with all the parishes where I had served represented, colleagues, Methodist and Anglican, and members of the family and the local community there as well. I presided at the Communion, and as I looked out, it was like a near-death experience, faces from the previous forty years mingled together, along with a thankful awareness of those "upon another shore, and in a greater light", to use the gentle phrase for the dead that came to mind.[119] My stipendiary ministry ended with an event that cast a retrospective light of blessing and appreciation over the years, something to treasure. Less rose-tinted narratives could have been constructed but there are few occupations that lend themselves to forming such attachments, or to such resonant celebrations.

The end of my fieldwork came at the same time, but I had no expectations of this being particularly marked at the gurdwara. I had previously been invited to use *chaur sahib*, to do the fly-swatting *seva* over *Guru Granth Sahib Ji*, something that anyone can do, including little children, but which I still appreciated. The associate membership idea had petered out. I prepared to finish, letting people know as a courtesy to my hosts, but not expecting a response. I asked Devsi what I could do to express my gratitude for their hospitality, and he recommended making a payment and asking for a prayer. I did this weekly, but now it was decided the prayer would be the *Sukhmani Sahib (Jewel of Peace)*, a blessing which takes a couple of hours. Usually this is done for a significant family event, with the fee being £51,[120] but people also pay for the food in the gurdwara as well, perhaps £500. £51 was manageable, £500 was not. Devsi discussed it with the committee and came back with the good news that they would like to pay it for me as a gift to mark my time with them. I expressed thanks, but insisted on paying the £51 as a sign of my own appreciation. I realized how unusual this was when the kitchen manager asked me about paying for the food. I told her what had been arranged, but she remained concerned until the president came over to reassure her. I never fully understood the financial arrangements but was not intended to, leaving me shielded from realizing how generously I was being treated and from the obligations to which this knowledge would have given rise.

Devsi had asked me to come early, so I was there for 9.30 a.m., while the gurdwara was still quiet. I paid my £51, and was again invited to go on *chaur sahib* duty, during which people were gradually filing in. When

I moved away from the *takhat* I went and sat near the front next to Devsi rather than at the back as normal. The chants went on, and I wondered at one point whether the prayers had started without me realizing, but at 10 a.m. prompt the attention switched to the *takhat*, where one of the *granthis* started to read. I had bought an English translation with which I tried to follow, but he finished well before I did. I found both the reading itself and my translation moving, feeling genuinely blessed. I was aware of Devsi sitting next to me and of how much I owed to him, and the general aura of generosity surrounding the event.

Considerable creativity had gone into dealing with this unprecedented relationship, so that the orbit of "welcome visitor" had been altered not by my attempts to unsettle it but by their (and which individuals were "they" was still not clear to me) generosity and inventiveness. I could hear people coming in as the gurdwara filled to its usual level of attendance, with men and women coming to greet me. The occasion was not entirely without hazard. As I sat there, I let my foot touch the translation, and Devsi urgently warned me against defilement of scripture, even if only an English version, and a friend who had noticed the faux pas brought me a small wooden bookstand to prevent it happening again. I was also achingly aware that I was sitting for the best part of four hours cross-legged, as normal prayers followed. Trying to maintain good posture and sit still got desperately uncomfortable, something which distracted from this most important spiritual and social event. However, the good wishes surrounding me continued as the stage secretary uttered kind words and a *granthi* presented me with a *siropa*, an honorific orange scarf. Devsi then made a wide-ranging speech, concluding that *Sikhi* has a precious message for the world and that he was delighted that I had come to find out about it and would be helping to spread it to others. He added that by now I knew more about *Sikhi* than many born Sikhs, and that I had got so engaged that I was considering taking *amrit*.

This sent me into confusion. I had previously ruled it out because according to the *Rehat Maryada* the taking of *amrit* required the denial of Jesus. Devsi had replied that such a denial was not part of the original meaning of *amrit*, but I had not taken this as suggesting that I move forward.[121] In fact, the lifestyle of dawn prayers, teetotalism and adopting the Five Ks was not something I was considering adopting. I was confused, and the short speech I had prepared got off to a sticky start as I had to deny that this was my intention and to reaffirm my loyalty to Christ as well as to the *sangat*. I denied any claim to expertise, saying that those who are born into *Sikhi* are the experts. I also picked up the theme of friendship, pointing out that both our masters greeted others with graciousness, and saying that our competitiveness on their behalf is just a sign of *manmukh*, self-centredness.

I stumbled through my speech, one of thanks and appreciation for hospitality and engagement throughout the time, thanking Devsi in particular and making a presentation to him, and explaining that not only had my fieldwork finished but that I had moved away so they would not see so much of me in future. It would have been possible to make a final break at that stage, but I realized I did not want to do so, nor to reject the many invitations to return. *Ardas* then followed, and when we came to the prayers I was moved to hear my name mentioned not just once in relation to my own donation but several times, indicating that a number of people had asked for prayers for me, with accompanying donations. Afterwards we went through to the *langar* hall and many people came over to greet me, including the president, who looked quite emotional. This had been a new experience, with, as usual, elements of uncertainty and of error, but mainly one for which I was very grateful, and I was now assured that they had appreciated my being with them.

After fieldwork

The sequel untidies the neat ending of the retirements and cessation of fieldwork and is a sign that what began then has continued to be important to me. My MRP is no longer a matter of research but is becoming an aspect of my own story, a story which ends in one way when I finish writing, in another, only on death or when memory of me has faded away.

The most obvious change on retirement was that much of my previous experience of Christian worship was in a leadership role and that this was a major concern when worshipping. I still attend Sunday worship and engage with it as much as, if not more than when leading. I have permission to officiate, and take some services in local churches, and a few for family and friends; I have also engaged with local organizations for retired clergy, being asked to convene the Birmingham retired clergy group. After three years I am still more aware of freedom than loss, though I acknowledge that balance could still change. My loyalties to the Christian faith and Church of England do not seem to have been damaged by my engagement with *Sikhi*. If anything they have been enhanced as I have been led to appreciate the generosity of Jesus and to expand my horizons as to how his (and Nanak's) own nature may hold a key to right interreligious relationships.

It was often in summer holidays that my desire and space to pray was rekindled, but retirement did not at first have that effect, and private prayer, Christian and Sikh, was reduced. I engaged in some intercessory prayer as a way of relating to the problems of others, and occasionally read the daily reading, *hukamnama*, from *Harmander Sahib* or from the Church of England's daily offices. I sometimes attended weekday prayers at the parish church or evening prayer at the cathedral, but without consistency. I wondered whether this was just taking a rest, or whether there was an unacknowledged depression underlying this inattentiveness, and if so, whether it came from retirement, or from spiritual confusion caused by MRP. I had to entertain the latter possibility although I did not feel it fitted. More positively, in October 2017 I noted about looking after grandchildren (of whom we have had five in four years) that when I started I used to think, "What on earth are we going to do for six hours?" but that time goes just like that. Perhaps there is a purity about the engagement and attention involved that is more wholesome than the self-conscious stuff of deliberate meditation. COVID-19 lockdown has changed the situation again, stopping physical participation in church and gurdwara and limiting contact with the children, but encouraging a renewed engagement with meditation, *hukamnama,* the daily offices, and intercessions.

As to my relationship with *Sikhi*, I chose a venue for *seva*, central Birmingham, which would be convenient when I retired, and kept that as a regular Monday engagement until the disruption of COVID-19. Friendships had grown as time passed, and I had my own regular role in the food line. I was still attending GKN gurdwara, until the COVID-19 lockdown, but in view of the distance and the varied times of church services I covered I only committed to going monthly. I was no longer wearing my clerical collar, nor did I have the distancing effect of being a researcher, so my participation felt more straightforward, but the loss of frequency seemed initially to loosen the relationship. After the first gap of three weeks people seemed busy about things of which I was no longer a part, though there were many greetings. My belonging felt diminished, a sign of those mundane reasons for reduced allegiance observable in many aspects of religious life. As to lifestyle, I have started to eat beef again when it is given to me, though I find I never choose it.

In August 2017 (a few weeks after the end of my fieldwork), I was invited to attend the opening of GKN's new *durbar*. It is no bigger than the old hall, but it does include a screen at the front. It is laid out the same except for an alcove to the right at the front, and at first it was used for major programmes while regular meetings still happened in the old hall. I was struck by the quality of the carpets, very soft and springy under foot. The place was full, and while I was there the mayor, MPs and councillors gradually came in and were seated, some on chairs at the back. The ceremony wended its way through several speeches, most in Punjabi, some in English, with one councillor fluent (so far as I could tell) in both. Then there were presentations of engraved plates to the dignitaries, during which the stage secretary called me up, "John Barnett . . . who used to be an officer", the last said uncertainly. I went up with a mixture of emotions, but mainly embarrassment. As the ceremony continued, I wondered why I had been troubled over something that I would once have taken in my stride. There was pleasure at being recognized in this way, something I had not realized I still desired, but also a feeling that I was once again a visitor, no longer the student but also not one of the hosts. I was back to where I was before, either as a reversion, as though nothing had happened in between, or as a restoration, a sign that I had not lost anything in the journey, but all had been gain. The feelings of loss and gain ran together and were equally strong.

Focal points

1. Meditation can generate a feeling of friendliness, demonstrating friendliness is not just a social experience but also a spiritual one, and it calls for attention from exponents of theology of religions.
2. The sense of stability, being held in orbit, identified in Chapter 3, proved open to further development, changing from event to event, decision to decision, and through developments in spiritual practice. There were also times of regression through error of practice and misunderstanding.
3. Belonging/not-belonging is not binary, but, both in its subjective and its communal aspects, varies in degree and type.
4. Obligation arises with belonging. My engagement with the tribunal felt like an obligation to those who asked me. My engagement with *seva* grew from a sense of obligation to express my *Sikhi* outside the gurdwara, to match spirituality and lifestyle.
5. My deliberately modest commitment to engagement with the gurdwara had an effect. It had affected them; they appreciated my engagement and showed their affection. It had also affected me; although I now have the chance to make a break I am not doing so.
6. The blanket of friendship was cast over many mistakes at the points of valediction in church and gurdwara. Corrections and instructions can build relationships if received gratefully.
7. Those born into faith are likely to have a thick cultural experience unavailable to the convert. This reflection came out of my rejection of Devsi's compliment comparing my knowledge with born Sikhs.
8. All three celebrations, interfaith, parish, and gurdwara, sketched stories of success and happiness (though others could have been written) and offered encouragement and blessing. I was holding them together as through me those celebrations mingled.
9. It is possible to change or reduce signs of commitment as circumstances change without weakening that commitment itself, something being widely demonstrated as I write this in isolation following the COVID-19 outbreak.

7

What's in a name?

As I progressed through the fieldwork, people asked me how I was getting on. How I replied was an attempt to tell them what was happening, but it also helped shape my own self-understanding. In particular, I had to consider what to call myself.

Nanak panthi

The *Rehat Maryada*'s veto on Sikhs owing "allegiance to any other religion" was a limiting factor for me as I had no wish to turn away from my Christian faith, and the restriction is intended to apply not just to *Amritdhari* but to any Sikh. When I realized this, I ceased to describe myself as Sikh. I looked back wistfully to a time when the demarcation was not so clear-cut, and started to call myself a *Nanak panthi*, a follower of Guru Nanak. A Christian with whom I was corresponding over her engagement in *Sikhi*, in which she had gone further than me, also decided to take the *Nanak panthi* identity rather than pursuing *amrit*, because of this need to forswear Christianity. Being *Nanak panthi* also distanced me from those *gora* who irritate Punjabi Sikhs by taking on the designation, outward appearance and spiritual practice of *Sikhi* while remaining distant from *Punjabiat*.

It was as a *Nanak panthi* that, at the end of 2016, after a year of research, I made a report to the gurdwara congregation, reading it out in the gurdwara and printing off copies which were all taken, with more still being requested weeks later. I also presented myself as a *Nanak panthi* in an article I was asked to write for *Mann Jitt Weekly*, which was republished in Interfaith Wolverhampton's newsletter, and which I sent to my bishop and to the *Presence and Engagement* national coordinator, generating encouraging responses. Being a *Nanak panthi* is a personal commitment to Guru Nanak, something that was growing on me. I wrote in the article:

> The more I hear and read about Guru Nanak Dev Ji the more I revere him and find his teachings attractive. [...] First, Guru Nanak's emphasis on non-discrimination in terms of religion, caste and gender, while consistent with Christianity, [... is] more clearly stated. Second, as I come to retirement, the model of Guru Nanak finishing his missionary journeys and settling down to the life of a householder appeals. Third, I find Guru Nanak easier to identify with than the later more communal and military tradition of Sikhism [...] Fourth, his criticism of [some religious practices of his day], like Jesus's criticism of [some religious practices in his context], strikes me as liberating.

I also expressed my continuing loyalty to Jesus, and in the face of the assumption that *karma*, one's true destiny, has to be channelled into just one religion, stated my conviction of a two-fold calling:

> I also remain committed to Jesus because knowing he gave his life for his friends is inspiring, his call for forgiveness is a way of changing the world, and his mysterious resurrection is a powerful sign that love is stronger than death. That and a lifetime's commitment to following him means there is no intention to break my loyalty to him in seeking to follow Guru Nanak as well, something that is appreciated by Sikh friends who would never encourage me to convert, but to follow the *hukam*[122] given me, this *hukam* of two-foldness.

Selective *Sikhi*

As indicated, one facet of this concentration on Guru Nanak was my hesitation over the more militaristic aspect of *Sikhi* which seemed to be a later tradition. At the Wolverhampton *Vaisakhi* celebrations, I watched young men and boys give martial arts displays, and heard children read about Sikh heroes killing hundreds of thousands of their adversaries; I have also seen young men unselfconsciously wearing Khalistan t-shirts illustrated with sub-machine guns. The readings were no worse than the Book of Judges, which I spiritualize or historicize without much reflection; I had taken part in rifle training as an Air Training Corps chaplain with only faint discomfort; and illustrations of the torture and deaths of Sikh heroes reminded me of the gory Christian martyrdoms that adorned the Spanish hotel rooms where I stayed as a child. A member of Beacon Church pressed for Mel Gibson's gruesome film of Jesus' crucifixion to be shown in church one Passiontide, something only prevented by (this time welcome to me) technical failure. It was not that I thought less of *Sikhi* because of these aspects or that they are alien to me as a Christian, but rather that I did not want to take on any more than I had already ingested.

However, my self-identifications as a Christian and a *Nanak panthi* were both challenged when I interviewed Inderjit Bhogal, interreligious activist and former president of the British Methodist Conference, about the relationship of the *Sikhi* into which he was born with Christianity. He affirmed his Sikh roots and added that he preferred to call himself a "follower of Christ" rather than a "Christian". He acknowledged his place in and need for the Christian community, but chose not to identify with all aspects of the historical Church, standing against its internal divisions, institutional inhumanity, and propensity to violence.[123]

There would have been a symmetry in my describing myself, like Bhogal, as a "follower of Christ", alongside being a *Nanak panthi*, both having a personal rather than an institutional focus, but then I thought that I was more drawn to be a "follower of Jesus" rather than "follower of Christ", as "Christ" is a title soaked in the theological speculation of the institution itself. At this point I began to lose confidence in Bhogal's approach, because this quibble had brought me up against the complex relationship between founder and later religion. The historical Jesus has been curated by the Church, even the Jesus of my own vision in 2007 was a cultural product, a gift of the Church; as a cradle Christian I was so utterly formed by the community that to claim otherwise was not an option. I could be selective about which aspects of that tradition I accepted, but all Christians select, some by individual discernment, all by cultural formation, and to identify all the attractive aspects of the faith with Jesus and all the difficult ones with the later Church is distorting and naïve.[124] On reflection it seemed that to refuse the description "Christian" was an unwarranted attempt to distance myself from the community in which I was formed and continue to be sustained.

My approach to *Sikhi* as a *Nanak panthi* was similarly challenged. The stories of Nanak's life, the *janam-sakhi*, had been gestating in oral traditions at least as long as the Christian gospels; the community at Kartarpur with *sangat* and *langar*, and the lineage of subsequent Gurus (or Nanaks), are both established by Nanak himself, rooting those continuing aspects of Sikh life in his teaching and example. The theory that Sikh militarism or the formation of the *Khalsa* was caused by an influx of *Jats* rather than the need of Guru Nanak's own community to preserve itself has been found wanting. Furthermore, my practical knowledge of *Sikhi* had come from the living *sangat*: it is with them I eat, worship, and ask questions. Any discernment I exercised could not be based on some unmediated source in the historical Guru; it related to the Sikh tradition as I had found it, historical, cultural, and political.

After further consideration I nonetheless decided to retain the description *Nanak panthi*, not now to distance myself from later aspects of *Sikhi*, but to indicate among Sikhs the space I am taking to acknowledge Christ, and to try to avoid *gora* presumptuousness.

Self-questionnaire

When I started my research, I decided to construct a simple monthly self-questionnaire and two of the questions addressed this issue of what I would call myself. I answered on a scale of 1–10 (10 being the highest) the degree to which I identified with two labels, "Sikh-Christian" and/or "Christian-Sikh". The use of a numerical scale is not intended to indicate some spurious objectivity, merely to enable me to track as well as I could my changes in attitude month by month as the research progressed.

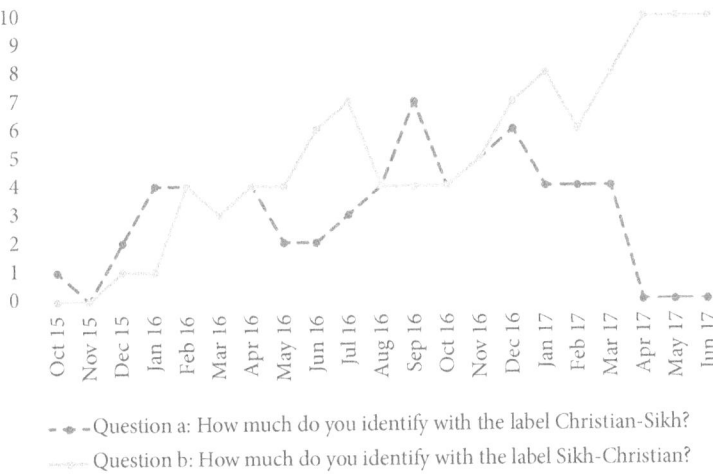

- ● - Question a: How much do you identify with the label Christian-Sikh?
  Question b: How much do you identify with the label Sikh-Christian?

Figure 1: Self-questionnaire: hyphenated identity.

I had not at the beginning thought through what the different labels might signify, though I recall that at an earlier stage I thought of myself as a Christian-Sikh, understanding "Sikh" as "student". I cannot account for the divergence that opens out in July 2016 nor the high value for "Christian-Sikh" in September 2016, and the graph does not show any effect of my adoption of the term *Nanak panthi*, which had occurred by December 2016. However, by April 2017, I had reached a settled preference for the label "Sikh-Christian", marking a clarified understanding of myself as still substantively Christian but with *Sikhi* as a qualifier, regarding "Christian" as the noun and the preceding "Sikh" as adjectival.[125]

Other questions were:

> On a scale of 1–10 where 1 is "not at all" and 10 is "completely":
> c. How loyal a Christian do you feel?
> d. How much do you identify with Sikhism?
> e. How easy are you finding it to practise the two religions?
> f. How much is practising two religions having an impact on how you live?
> g. How much would you recommend anyone else to try this?

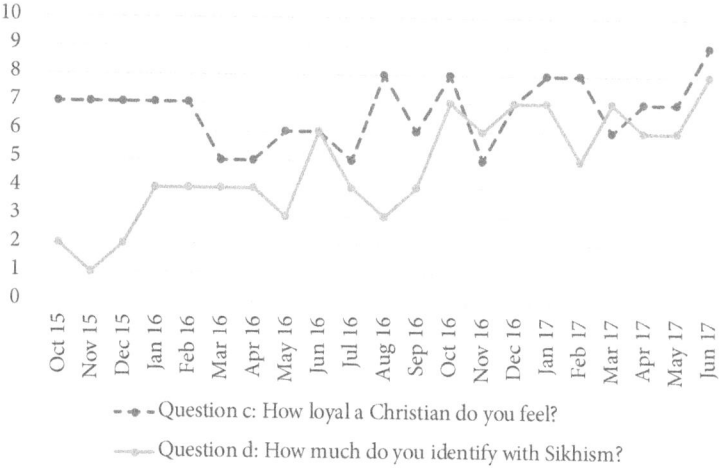

- - Question c: How loyal a Christian do you feel?
— Question d: How much do you identify with Sikhism?

Figure 2: Self-questionnaire: loyalty and identification.

The different style of questions c and d reflected my starting point of rootedness in Christianity and freshness to Sikhism (as I then called *Sikhi*). Overall there is a slight improvement in Christian loyalty and a marked improvement in Sikh identity, though this may just signify my desire that the research be worthwhile. The dip in identification with Sikhism in November 2015 was when the first gurdwara rejected my request to research there, and the recovery in January coincided with the approval at GKN. The dip in May 2016 coincided with discussions that month on Sikh antipathy to *Ek Niwas* temple, and with the *Ravidassi* outburst on Sikh caste consciousness. I also see in my notes (26 May) "bored for the first time at the gurdwara", the only recording of boredom throughout the fieldwork. The recovery in June is matched by a note: "Feel more Sikh again. Using *Waheguru* in meditation suddenly feels more natural . . . I am coping with the physical thing of praying." The divergence in August 2016 reflects Peter's illness and my grasping at a Christian identity in response. The November 2016 dip in Christian loyalty coincides with a time of exploring the transcendentalist view that specific religious identities are not significant. After that, there is a higher level in both religious identifications moving toward the positive conclusion of fieldwork and ministry.

WHAT'S IN A NAME?

I explored my engagements with the two religions, which increased and which decreased, month by month.

Year	2015		2016													2017					
Month	N	D	J	F	M	A	M	J	J	A	S	O	N	D	J	F	M	A	M	J
Qc (Christian)	-	-	-	-	↓	-	↑	-	↓	↑	↓	↑	↓	↑	↓	-	↓	↑	-	↑
Qd (Sikh)	↓	↑	↑	-	-	-	↓	↑	↓	↓	↑	↑	↓	↑	-	↓	↑	↓	-	↑

Figure 3: Monthly movements in engagement with Christianity and *Sikhi*.

There were three months where neither loyalty to Christianity or *Sikhi* changed, and seven months where only loyalty to the one religion altered. Where both loyalties changed, there were five months where loyalty to one went up and the other down, but there were also five months where they went up or down together. This is significant because if I had found myself making a stark choice between religions there might be expected to be a clear pattern of my loyalty to Christianity going down as my loyalty to *Sikhi* went up and vice versa. There is no such indication, suggesting that I was not experiencing the two religions as competitors.

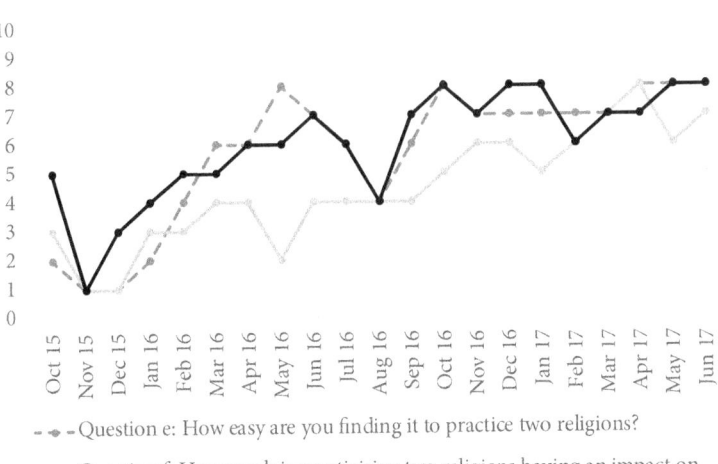

- - ● - - Question e: How easy are you finding it to practice two religions?
──○── Question f: How much is practicing two religions having an impact on how you live?
──●── Question g: How much would you recommend anyone else to try this?

Figure 4: Self-questionnaire: practising two religions.

All three questions received more positive answers at the end of the fieldwork than at the beginning. The dip in November 2015 across all questions reflected the rejection at the first gurdwara. The divergence in May 2016, where I was finding my practise of *Sikhi* easy but it was having little impact, suggests I had established a manageable rhythm but that it was no longer having its first impact. I also note that in May I met—and in some cases interviewed—people from multi-faith families who found their own MRP normal and easy. The fall in willingness to recommend MRP and in ease of practice in August 2016 coincided with Peter's illness and reflected my reaction to it. It was not until October 2016 that the effect on my life of MRP reached the mid-point, 5. I cannot explain the upturn then but the increase in April 2017 coincides with my involvement in *seva* in Birmingham.

Self-description revisited

In July 2017, I retired and moved house, having to register at the local doctor's where the registration form included the opportunity to identify my religion. I ticked the "Christian (Anglican)" box, and wondered if I should tick the "Sikh" box as well. It seemed presumptuous, bearing in mind my still very limited acclimatization to *Sikhi* and how inappropriate it would seem to some religious purists and Punjabi nationalists, but against that was a counter-pull, a sense that my relationships with GKN and the *seva* group, and to a lesser extent with *Sikhi* more widely, gave a reality to my relationship that I was loath to ignore. I left it to think about but had forgotten to resolve the issue by the time I took the form back. When I later realized I had not ticked the "Sikh" box, I had an unexpectedly keen sense that I had let down, betrayed even, my friends. I went back to the doctor's again for an introductory appointment, and when the receptionist got my notes up on her screen I took the chance to ask if she would alter them to indicate my Sikh identity as well as the Christian one. I felt embarrassed doing this in a white suburban village, and with no sign of my *Sikhi* apart from a (trimmed) beard. "There, that's done!" she said after a moment, and anxiety was replaced by a peaceful exhilaration.

Two weeks later I renewed my registration at the university. There was a drop-down box for "religion" in the equalities monitoring section, and there was no option to indicate any form of MRP, just single mainstream religions or "any other religion", a reminder that MRP does not easily fit such statistical monitoring. As I ticked the "Christian" box, I remembered the comments on my turban-wearing photograph from the Jordanian student, remarking on the religious fixity in her society. It demonstrated that institutions, like states and religious hierarchies, are more comfortable with monolithic religious descriptions, and that evidence of MRP—sometimes MRP itself—is likely to be suppressed in many environments.

Focal points

1. Members of any widespread religion are selective about which aspects of that tradition they accept, some by individual discernment, all by cultural formation. Being selective does not prevent belonging.
2. When describing myself my reply may vary depending on context, sometimes identifying as *Nanak panthi*, sometimes as Sikh-Christian, sometimes as just Christian. This varies according to the person I am addressing and the context of the discussion as I seek to reflect my self-understanding as closely as possible. These different descriptions must be managed carefully to avoid accusations of being two-faced.
3. This points to something obvious but often overlooked, that many people have a "near enough" description of themselves, but can qualify or flex that in many ways.
4. The self-questionnaire confirms modern cognitive dissonance theory in that questions b) and c) suggest loyalty to Christianity and identification with *Sikhi* are not conflicted. I am not shown as consistently torn between them.
5. People may be subtle in describing their own religion, but institutions by and large are not, and being threatened or confused by those subtleties, refuse to recognize them. This hides the extent of MRP and smaller faiths.

8

Changing interfaith practice

The study of religions

The fluidity and complexity of belonging is only just beginning to receive widespread attention in the study of religions. What is recognized is that how long someone has been involved, how much they know about beliefs and practices, their spiritual depth, and their seniority in a religious organization may all be related but still fail to produce a clear picture of how much that person really belongs. In the face of this complexity, "system of reference", "allegiance", "affinities", or "preferences" have been used in describing the relationship with religion instead of "belonging". Whichever way that connection is described, however, there is a further, less-recognized factor to consider: that is, the connection often changes over time. There is likely to be some fluctuation going on, perhaps dramatic, perhaps long-term, for individuals and for whole societies.

Throughout my fieldwork the participation was constant while belonging fluctuated, something that produced a narrative tension. Would belonging to the gurdwara and *Sikhi* develop, and would belonging to the church, Beacon or Christianity more widely diminish? The only answer is the story itself; I deliver a narrative verdict because any "conclusions" would be as continually changing as the experience itself. By varying the point at which the story stops, at the end of different chapters for example, different conclusions can be drawn, and, despite my pleasure at a positive outcome, the happy ending of Chapter 6 is as arbitrary a finishing point as any other. Factors affecting the changes in the level of belonging include (with examples):

- formal religious structures (*amrit*, gurdwara membership, ordination, Methodist ministers not being congregation members);
- social factors (language and cultural aspects at the gurdwara, unwritten expectations on circuit);
- passage of time (my short posting at Beacon Church, the "new place" arising at the gurdwara after seeming stuck as welcome visitor);
- spirituality and way of engaging (acceptance of cognitive dissonance);
- circumstances (Peter's illness, retirement);
- inherent attitudes of religious groups (hospitality at the gurdwara, mutual support at Beacon Church, anxiety of colleagues);
- personal relationships (creative and accepting friendliness at church and gurdwara, as shown in farewells);
- chance (the tribunal engagement).

Along with the variation in my belonging over time the position at the end of the period is by no means clear-cut, as demonstrated by the tick-box conundrum at surgery and university; a *Nanak panthi* is neither a proper Sikh, nor not-a-Sikh.

This is a long way from the simple models of belonging that have been assumed in much religious discourse and in the study of religions even where MRP is being acknowledged. Likely causes for oversimplification are the frequency of examples being taken from the unconsidered ease of MRP as an accepted part of the culture as in many Eastern settings, or from the simplicity and potential privacy of "taking refuge" where Buddhism is a second religion, a popular choice among Western explorers. Both of these mask the nuances faced by someone making a deliberate choice to engage with two enfleshed religious communities. Such deliberate, chosen community-crossing is taking place, however. Karen Thompson gives examples of a Christian-Muslim, Anne Holmes Redding, and a Jewish-Christian, Deborah Risa Mrantz, to whom could be added the Hindu-Christian David Hart, and I had no difficulty in finding people to interview whose lives were in some way Sikh and Christian. Such combinations may be very easy, but they can also generate their own fruits and problems.

Meetings with interfaith advisers

MRP is not just an academic issue, but is a matter of continued judgement for those involved in interreligious relationships and particularly for those charged with giving advice on the subject. I have referred to the Church of England's call to caution over joining in the prayers of other religions, the warnings of the World Council of Churches in the context of a more positive approach, and Catholic encouragement to well-grounded Christians to share in the spiritual riches of other religions. Advice from practitioners ranges from a clear warning against joining in prayer to full participation in Ramadan. These variations point to a need for the subtlety and courage of professional practice rather than reliance on a rulebook. Donald Schön in his classic work, *The Reflective Practitioner*, examined reflection-in-action (at the time) and reflection-on-action (in retrospect) in a number of different professional settings, neither reducing it to an easily learned technical skill nor elevating it to the mysterious priestcraft of an elite.[126] Professional wisdom arises from experience, from implicit understandings and from experimentation. It needs to take into account the wider social context and is unlikely to produce an off-the-shelf solution, and it cannot afford to become so complex that it paralyses action.

With my retirement I have ceased to be an active DIFA but my approach is that of a participating associate, experimenting on former colleagues' behalf and encouraged by the interest they have shown, rather than that of a complete outsider offering advice. I have these former colleagues particularly in mind as I write this chapter, though the research is intended to be of use to anyone engaged in or interested in interreligious activity, professional or voluntary. The marginal nature of the DIFA in institutional terms and my own retired liberty combine to allow a radical approach, not criticizing those who are more cautious but offering my own decisions and experience for consideration and judgement by others.

In May and July 2017, towards the end of my fieldwork, I convened two focus groups with DIFAs and people in related roles or with similar interests, including some with regional roles and one non-Anglican. Each group was composed of four people and myself and the discussions both extended well over the hour for which I had asked. One group was composed entirely of older men; the other was more mixed in age and included two women. All were white British. Both groups knew each other beforehand and the atmosphere was relaxed, frank, and consensual. The intent of any focus group is to promote some self-disclosure among participants, but this was balanced in this case by the need to protect participants, so requests to edit the draft notes of the meeting were all complied with, and individual speakers have not been identified. At both meetings I shared my research interest and then asked about any experiences participants may have had of joining in the worship of other religions, and their reflections. They were generous enough to offer emotional engagement as well as the intellectual comment that sometimes characterizes such groups.[127] There was no marked difference in the overall response of the two groups, and the following points emerged.

Outcomes of discussions

a) Sometimes attendance at non-Christian worship was worthwhile purely as a sign of fellowship without the need for prayerful participation:

> I think going to [the] ... mosque I am going there as an empathetic presence, mostly [...] I sit in my dog-collar right at the back trying to say [...] "I want to show that I am on your side, and we are all people of faith."

b) However, participants did sometimes find themselves caught up in non-Christian worship:

> I share and feel that I am caught up in the yearning for God which is being expressed through whatever form, and that can be Hindu pilgrims walking in and throwing butter-packs at the

> statue [...] seeing the Torah being taken in procession and the desire to touch it, and the Islamic music and the call to prayer. For me there is something really profound, really moving about that.
>
> I feel I am caught up in it [Muslim worship], even though I am stood at the back, and I am so impressed by the atmosphere.
>
> Some of the most profound moments I have had have been listening to [...] Sufi music.
>
> It's not that I believe in Hindu doctrines ... but the worship feeds me ... it's something to do with the atmosphere.
>
> (Interviewee:) There was something about the yoga ... when we first started the chanting I had no idea what the words meant ... but you can see the translation ... and I realized that the chants are the kind of thing that anyone who believes in God ... would be comfortable with ... I thought, "How is this different from the rosary or doing the Jesus prayer? It isn't."

c) This gave rise to some self-questioning: "But then that's me psychologically or empathetically feeling at home with this, but is that quite the same as saying that theologically?"

> If you are taking a Christian perspective, do you have to pray with the words 'through Christ our Lord'?

d) A sense of restraint as a Christian limited engagement: "I am also conscious of my own Christian identity and therefore in a sense I feel it is incumbent on me to be slightly separate from that."

> I am trying to be open to what aspect of God the people who are worshipping are being open to ... but I think ... how far can you do that?

e) The roles of participant and reserved observer can oscillate or be experienced simultaneously:

> You find yourself at one stage as a participant caught up in it and at other stages, in fact in minutes sometimes, as an observer, and I think it oscillates between the two so often. . . . Empathy is the word, not sympathy but real empathy.

> If I can have a refereeing analogy you may see something going on but then you are concentrating on the game, and then later on you say, 'I saw that . . .'. It's going with the flow but also realizing that there is something going on in one's own mind . . . trying to work out what is going on in my own relationship with God.

f) The word of Jesus may be recognized even where he is not named: "The crunch point is: does Jesus have to be named as 'Jesus' or can it just be the Word?"

> If you say, 'in the name of Jesus', that means 'this is a prayer Jesus would have prayed.' . . . If it ties in with the Lord's Prayer, I am happy to say 'amen' to it.

g) Discernment was holistic, drawing on prior knowledge of the religion concerned, especially where there was a language issue:

> I don't know any Punjabi or Gurmukhi . . . but I read the *Guru Granth Sahib Ji* in translation, [and] a lot of it reminds me of the Hebrew prophets; I feel there is an awful lot in common . . . and therefore if you are there in the gurdwara and hearing that singing you know it is that kind of praise that is going on, even if you don't understand a word of it.

> I don't understand Arabic, but the language isn't a barrier, you can sometimes detect a pattern of where you are, where you're going.

I will pray, but I don't pray the liturgy probably, because I don't understand it.

That smidgeon of Punjabi that I have enables me to join in with those prayers of intercession with the good Lord being asked to support Mrs So-and-so who is going in for a hospital appointment, and I am thinking, 'Yes I'm there with you.'

However, another participant commented:

Where I personally struggle to engage with worship is if I am in a context where I don't understand the language, and therefore it is hard to maintain focus for a long time ... if I can't join in the corporateness of it I start to disengage.

h) Actions drew forth special consideration:

Being asked to put a garland on Gandhi, I think: "Well, fine, this may not be what I normally do, but clearly it would be impolitic to refuse and I don't actually have a problem with this."

I would not go and join a line of prayer, but I would quite happily pray to God in my own head.

If someone gave me an *aarti*[128] plate, I would quite happily move my hands over the flames, because I understand the theology behind it.

Where they all start doing *puja*[129] ... they say "No you don't want one of these" ... and you think, "Fine, that's your choice you made for me. I'm not getting into an argument about that."

I think I would distinguish very much between joining in the five times daily prayers *salaat*[130] standing on the end of the line, I have never considered doing that because that is a bit like somebody from another faith participating in the Eucharist. It is the thing that shows the identity of that faith . . .

They wanted me to bathe the Buddha. I felt very unhappy doing that. One of the reasons was that they *expected* me to do that and I felt that I was being forced into a situation that I was not comfortable with as a representative of the Christian Church.

i) Images were not presented as a problem:

A German friend of mine talked in terms of "übersehen" [. . .] we would use the term "to see through", and I was able to relate to the meaning of the image rather than the image *per se*.

I think it's very similar when going to benediction and you have the host and you are seeing Christ as somehow present in that bread, and you say that for the Hindus, God is somehow present in that image, and being empathetic to that and maybe to bow towards that image and be respectful towards it, realizing that it's a little face of God.

Among all the Hindu Gods at the front of the room . . . there was a crucifix, there was a Madonna and Child, there was an empty cross and a Christian icon, so I found that reassuring because clearly they weren't catering purely for the people who were going to the Hindu root . . .

j) Worship participation was reduced when exercising public roles as Christian representatives, particularly leading groups. This was motivated by, and had consequences for, relationships:

I would never join with their [Sufi] group when they are meeting publicly—they meet in a church—because I think it creates an issue for me in terms of my identity. I am very happy to join in privately and I get caught up in the meditation they practise and share it with them, but I would be very wary about doing it publicly.

If I took a group [. . .] to a mosque we wouldn't in any way join in [. . .] for me personally it's more complicated if I am the sole person.

I will often not receive [*karah parshad*] as a sign that it's fine not to . . .

The Sikh guide will normally say, "I'm going to bow to *Guru Granth Sahib Ji* out of respect. You don't have to but you can," leaving it to other people, but because I'm meant to be this almost neutral guide and facilitator I deliberately don't bow, but if I was going on my own I would sit and I would sing maybe.

It might be their first experience of a different place of worship, a Christian, and they are so terrified by what they might encounter [. . .] so that if I started to participate they would freak out even more.

The only other role that I'm really cautious with apart from my own role is if I was taking members of the congregation from [my spouse's] church [. . .] I worry a lot of people may have a problem with me worshipping in a Hindu context.

On the other hand, their role or the needs of the group could lead to more engagement rather than less:

If you are the chaplain or something, then to a certain extent you have to embrace and engage with and help people who are not of your tradition. We talk about it with the group beforehand, and say, "Only do what you're comfortable with," but if the leader doesn't do it then in a way that inhibits those who want to do it. I can see exactly what you mean [in not participating] but you can play it either way.

k) Both focus groups independently and unprompted raised alienation arising in Christian worship, sometimes more than with other faiths:

> Can I be provocative and say the only group I feel uncomfortable with are certain kinds of Christians? I feel if you know you're a visitor in another faith, that relaxes you because if there is something going on you're not quite sure of, you're not being expected to be committed to that, whereas if you go into some Christian environments you feel that whoever is leading it or the people round about you expect you to be committed to that and if you're not, that's when I feel uncomfortable.

> I would want to bring in other Christian worship here as part of that spectrum because when one goes to Roman Catholic mass in this country I am trying to pray but conscious that I am not fully part of it, and similarly if I go to an Evangelical church with bands and what have you again I am trying to be present, I am trying to be empathetic, but it really isn't my tradition, so there is a limit to how I can actually engage. Then one goes to a synagogue and I feel much more at home, especially with the Psalms, and even if the Psalms are being sung in Hebrew I can follow the Psalms in the book as though I am saying the office at home.

> Some of the prayers I hear in a Christian context, we had an ecumenical gathering where [...] some of the things that were being prayed for I felt profoundly this is not a prayer Jesus would have prayed and I cannot say "amen" to this.

l) Issues of theology of religion were addressed in different ways; agreement in practice did not always come from a shared theological perspective: "'They are all wrong and we are all right' ... unless you are going to take that perspective ... it's a challenge to you. So the theological questions pile up."

> I went to a Christian ashram and it turned out that actually what I thought it was about Hindu worship that attracted me so much ... actually existed in Christianity and I had no idea.

> With Buddhism it is perfectly within reason to be able to view one's life with a foot in both camps.

> The engagement with other scriptures can help us appreciate our own scriptures.... When we engage with other scriptures there are echoes of our own scriptures in our minds and then we have echoes of those scriptures when we engage with ours.

> I tend to analyse my response to human nature and my response to what's going on very much through a mixture of Sikh and Christian eyes ... I found myself ... within the sermon using Sikh texts.

> The other is there to challenge me but not just to challenge me, it's actually to draw me out, and I think there is a sense in my identity that actually grows and is enriched by facing the different.

> I am increasingly of the opinion that we all have our different narratives, and it is the way of expressing our identity, but in the end, there is a sense in which collectively we are yearning for the same.

> People assume that because I'm very happy to partake in Hindu worship then I'm a pluralist. If I pigeon-hole myself into a particular box it wouldn't be that one. It's not that I believe in any Hindu doctrines, I don't believe in reincarnation if you like, or in karma, but the worship feeds me, but that certainly doesn't mean I would describe myself as a Hindu-Christian ...

The interviewee commented:

> If it was something that was purely secular ... a relaxation group or something like that, I don't think it would worry me at all, and there is no reason why something that comes from a different religious perspective should automatically be any more threatening ...

A commentary

Among interfaith colleagues I was aware that I had taken a step a number of them would have hesitated over in joining in Sikh worship, but none condemned it, and most acknowledged that they had prayed in non-Christian places of worship without being entirely clear whether that prayer was exclusively Christian or not;[131] this was something I had experienced myself and recognized from others, including those from Beacon Church who visited GKN. Most focus group members had held back from full participation in worship of another faith, by gesture or mental reservation, restrained for doctrinal reasons or in their specific role as clergy or interfaith advisers (or a lecturer on religions). It was the first time any focus group members had engaged in sustained discussion of the issue, and they were not confident in the discernment involved.

Whether and how much to participate is partly a matter of empathy or psychology (c).[132] As one participant commented in a previous interview:

> Work ... [needs] to be done on the psychology of the people who are involved with interfaith dialogue ... What is it that means some people who have multiple religious participation can deal with the insecurity that brings?

It is also tied up with a discernment that (following Schön's distinction) uses both reflection-in-action to make decisions at the time, and the later reflection-on-action, to draw on the experience later to enhance understanding. This discernment is Christ-focussed[133] but not Christian-limited; the key question concerns compatibility with the teachings and examples of Jesus (f), and is a holistic judgement which takes into account the adviser's fullest extent of knowledge and experience of the faith concerned (g). Christians need to be well-grounded in their own faith, and have real—however modest—knowledge of the community on which they are seeking discernment. The discernment required does not so much rest on a generalized concept of religion but needs to reflect the complexity of lived religion with its unending range of beliefs and practices, and it invites a level of engagement that may change the person concerned. The subtlety of the discernment reaches beyond labels, shown in the focus groups (k) by their experience of some Christian worship as not only less appealing but also less true to Jesus than some worship of other religions. Those with whom I was speaking did not feel that they had the confidence of the wider church in any cross-religious prayer, and felt that making public even unsought experiences risked distressing, angering, or confusing other Christians (j).

An exhortation

In response I would claim from my experience that becoming involved in the worship of other religions is not a minor or worrying by-product of interfaith work but a significant gift to the Church. The engagement of DIFAs, often in part-time roles or with no allocated time at all, and circumscribed by the conventions of church life, may not seem much, but few others in the UK take part in interreligious activity with the Christian rootedness and the professional wisdom of my former colleagues, and the call to "share [. . .] spiritual riches, e.g. regarding prayer"[134] is one few are better equipped to follow. Specific professional benefits have arisen from my research experience:

i) It has raised the whole issue of spiritual discernment, not exhausted by discovering and abiding by religious boundaries, but calling for more subtle judgement, piercing between joints and marrow (Hebrews 4:12). This is something which DIFAs need to hone because they should be able to offer help in this to others.

ii) It has brought to the surface the issue of prayer with other faiths as a complex relationship, sometimes Christian but in another faith setting, sometimes a partnership in prayer, sometimes no longer distinct from the prayer context in which it is taking place. Prayer can be both the guardhouse of particularity and the gateway of solidarity and DIFAs need their advice to match this fluid reality.

iii) It has brought into focus the lives of that growing number of people who live across religions, noted by the Church of England's General Synod and likely to give rise to situations where DIFAs are expected to offer advice.

These are all reasons why DIFAs should relate to the worship of another religion at greater depth than the scattergun visits necessary for retaining a wide range of contacts. Circumstances, theology, and personal inclination will affect how colleagues approach such boundary-crossing, but I encourage them to be more intentional in such steps, and the Church to support such initiatives and hear what is reported back. This will require a significant change for the Church because rejection of the testimony of those who are deeply engaging with other faiths is a long-standing problem. Someone who had been working as a Christian missionary in the Indian subcontinent in the 1970s told me that he, along with a number of his colleagues, came to appreciate and respect the faiths they were dealing with, but this attitude had to be moderated or even suppressed in reporting back to their supporters and funders in the UK. This was a pattern found in missionary endeavours for at least a century before that.

Church discomfort in the face of Christians finding anything nourishing and beneficial in other religious traditions continues, as was shown in the 2019 decision to withdraw the hospitality of York Minster from a Zen group run by Christopher Collingwood, one of the canons there, following criticism from evangelical Anglicans that its presence was deceptive and dishonouring to Jesus. This was despite the facts that Collingwood's book, *Zen Wisdom for Christians*, which argues that the practice of Zen can lead Christians towards deeper spirituality, had its launch party at the Minster's chapter house a few months before, and that the book remained on sale in the Minster shop after the group was told to move out.[135]

A graphic example of this confusion is the earlier case of Anne Holmes Redding, an Episcopalian priest for twenty-three years with a doctorate from Union Theological Seminary, who in 2007 announced that she had been called by Jesus to make the *shahada*, the Muslim testament of faith, and now considered herself fully Muslim as well as fully Christian. Her interim bishop said that he accepted her as an Episcopalian priest and a Muslim and found the interfaith possibilities exciting. However, when a new diocesan bishop was appointed, Redding was inhibited (suspended), and eventually deposed (defrocked), as the bishop did not believe a priest of the church could be both Christian and Muslim despite finding Redding a woman of utmost integrity and their conversations open, honest, and respectful.[136] The legal sticking point was Redding having being admitted into a religious body not in communion with the Episcopal Church, but priests who become Quakers or even those who take refuge as Buddhists have not been so sanctioned. Her sanction was only related to her priesthood; there was no excommunication and she continued to worship without hindrance as an Anglican lay person. A traditionalist commentator on the bishops' responses said of the Episcopalian Church, "we are internally incoherent on a massive scale."[137]

Perhaps if either bishop had been a practical theologian they might have said, Gamaliel-like[138]: "My initial reaction is that I [accept/cannot accept] Redding's position, but recognizing the growing significance of MRP, and her own ministerial maturity, theological acumen and integrity, the Church will seek to learn from her about the possibilities and difficulties as they unfold rather than foreclosing in judgement." If Redding's role was that of a bishop's DIFA with the very task of exploring interreligious relationships, a restrained but attentive episcopal response would have been even more appropriate. Such boundary-testing is not a niche matter but is important for the nature of Christian identity and how it—and other religious identities—may continue to re-form in the decades to come.

Focal points

1. Religious (and other) belonging is complex and potentially fluid, with narrative often being the best way, and sometimes the only way, to describe that complexity and fluidity.
2. DIFAs sometimes find themselves caught up in non-Christian worship despite anxiety about what other Christians would think.

3. Evaluation of that participation requires a discernment as to how Christlike the worship is. Similar practice in this field did not necessarily flow from identical theology.
4. DIFAs have had no encouragement to reflect on this issue from the wider Church.
5. The discernment required does not rest on a generalized concept of religion but needs to reflect the complexity of lived religion. The subtlety of the discernment reaches beyond labels, as shown by problems engaging with some Christians.
6. DIFAs need to be able to offer advice on these subtle issues and so should be encouraged by the Church in their own exploration and reflection. The Church should hear in a context of critical support what they have to say as a matter affecting its own identity.

9
An imaginative interlude

Having begun my engagement with MRP because making friends across religions did not seem enough on its own, it was ironic to find friendliness had become such a motif of my meditative experience in the gurdwara that it required renewed theological attention. I wanted to express this experience but was not sure how to go about it; it was an important feeling but at that stage had no clear meaning or concepts attached. In a holiday immediately after the fieldwork, I set out to develop a clearer image of what I was experiencing by sketching Jesus and Nanak as friends, and by writing fourteen short pieces, one each morning, imagining them together with me at various points in their ministries. Such imagination is not just daydreaming but is a way of entering the world of inner vision which can be an instrument of God, and it helps to make sense of experience, not being alien to reason but functioning differently. I am using it to shape the raw meditative sensation so that I can develop an appropriate theology, a theology nourished by the imagination and with an imaginative power of its own.

The Sketch

As to the drawing, I wanted some way of attending to the friendship between Jesus and Nanak alongside theological speculation and the practical outworking of friendship across faiths, to sketch Nanak and Jesus walking together, and then to imagine them present in each other's stories, with me there as well. This creative attempt was something playful, suitable for a holiday, and the chance came in a setting that felt impossibly decadent. We were based in a Spanish villa, two married couples, with a 1/3 acre garden of olives, grapes, limes, pomegranates, and fruits of Sharon. We had an outside seating area where I wrote and drew.

Figure 5: Nanak and Jesus walking together. Author's sketch.

It was important to me to establish equality between the figures, so neither of them was talking or gesticulating to the other but both just walking along together. Why walking rather than sitting? I liked the dynamic nature of this. I also wanted a balance, and took as a model a photograph of friends walking together where one was leading but the other was in the foreground. I tried to place their heads at the same height and at the same distance from the centre of the field. I wanted to portray them at about the same age, inevitably younger than many pictures of Nanak but I wanted to get as near to an historical picture of both figures as I could, drawing on the internet for some suggestions as to their physical appearances and the clothing they may have worn.

I was aware of the risk of offence to both communities. Although pictures of Nanak are a commonplace in Sikh literature and in gurdwaras, I knew of the uproar over his depiction in the animated film *Nanak Shah Fakir*, and that there is growing sensitivity about depictions of the Guru. I was also aware of the botched restoration of the picture of Jesus in Borja and the derision to which that had given rise, so knew I was entering on risky holy ground in a very amateurish way, but there were two prizes to be had. One was a time of concentration in a different way on Nanak and Jesus and the relation between them, with its possibility of new understanding; the other was the likelihood that this was the first picture of Jesus and Nanak together. There are plenty where they are in a row of portraits with other faith leaders, but this, for all its laughable amateurism, would be something different, with its depiction of relationship.[139]

Imaginative writing

As to the imaginative work, this is based very loosely on the Ignatian exercise of imagining oneself in the presence of Jesus, and what he might say to you. Following that Ignatian approach I sought to use my imagination not just to connect "with ancient [gospel] events, but also [as] the event of direct contact with God".[140] The title of the last Ignatian exercise, *Contemplation to Attain Love*, summarizes the aim, an aim motivated by the sense that God is waiting to reveal himself. In seeking to insert Nanak and Jesus in each other's stories and see how that worked out, I had to decide how to choose my stories over the fourteen mornings of the holiday. I tried to have a more historical basis for the scenes, and so chose them from *The Gospel of Jesus according to the Jesus Seminar*, which claimed to offer a consensus of views as to the historical likelihood of stories about him, and from *The Book of Nanak*, which seeks to place some of the traditional stories in as precise a historical framework as possible.[141] I worked through them chronologically, but then jumped ahead to the passion and resurrection (neither in the Jesus Seminar text) and the retirement of Nanak. There were times where loneliness was a part of the story. This I felt applied particularly to the temptation and crucifixion of Jesus, and so Nanak leaves him at those times, entering into his own experience of loneliness as the relationship is sustained through the parting.

Nanak's thread-tying

Jesus and I are at Nanak's *yajnoparavitam*, his Hindu thread-tying ceremony. We are eleven or twelve years old. We are among his friends, behind the relatives, all bustling about, but being careful to step round the sacred signs drawn on the floor. I am still standing at the back, but Jesus has moved through the crowd to the front row. Something is going wrong. The crowd has gone quiet, someone gasps, and then everyone seems to be talking at once with some voices raised in anger, though I can see Jesus now, and he is not saying anything. Nanak, it seems, has refused to wear the thread.

Later on, we are left together as the adults, despite events, are busy about the celebrations. "How did they take it?" asks Jesus, because Nanak's parents had taken him away for a quiet word.

"Oh, you know," says Nanak. "It's hard for parents when they see us opening up to the divine."

I say, "I keep quiet about it, but you two just lay it out. Do you remember [to Jesus] when you told your parents that the Temple was your real home? That didn't go down too well."

"Yes," says Jesus. "According to our parents, I'm too religious and you [looking at Nanak] aren't religious enough!"

Nanak at the temptations of Jesus

Jesus is tempted to prove he is God's son. Nanak is standing next to me watching, but hidden from Jesus:

> He needs to be on his own, for this is his victory. He is revealing his *Dharma*,[142] turning away from these temptations of the ego, spiritual and worldly. The irony is these events will be seized on by his followers to promote him in just those egotistical terms, and so promote themselves of course.

Then the temptations were finished, and slipping in with the angels, Nanak sped to bring Jesus nourishment. Jesus greeted him: "We'll both of us have divinity force-fed to us if they have their way."

Nanak put an arm round him: "You saw them off!"

"For the time being. They'll be back, for us both."

The children come to Jesus

The disciples are stopping some family groups. The families are talkative and a bit rowdy; some are desperate. The word has got round that a blessing for your child from Jesus has great power. They have been getting in the way of people with serious needs for healing and deliverance and now they are disrupting Jesus' rest periods too. The disciples are letting a few of those serious adult enquirers through, and I am about to go with them, but Nanak stops me: "Let's wait here with the children." I protest there is no sign they are going to let the children past, but then Jesus calls out to the disciples not to stand in their way. The children rush towards him like an unblocked stream, but become calm as they get nearer to him. He talks with them and blesses them as the hubbub dies down, then he spots Nanak and myself among the families and gives him a smile: "Are you still a child in all your wisdom, my friend?"

"I still meditate as I did when I was grazing the family buffaloes."

They both laugh, remembering Nanak's boyhood career as an absent-minded herdsman. "I can see you there as you speak, and the buffaloes wandering off into the neighbour's field."

"Then you will see that no harm was done."[143]

"None at all, none at all," agrees Jesus, and again they both laugh, before Jesus turns back to the children, giving them once more his full attention.

Nanak's period of listlessness

Nanak's family is worried. I have called by at the house with Jesus. Nanak is in the back room, withdrawn, and eating and drinking very little. We join the family as they discuss the doctor's diagnosis (they were "not to worry. Nanak is not an ordinary person but a great being"). But worry they do, about "sickness of the soul", which is the only way they can understand this. Will it just go of its own accord or should the doctor be giving him some special treatment? Is the doctor being a bit too casual about it? I support his reassurance to the parents, trying to cheer them up by speculating about what sort of "great" Nanak will be.

I notice Jesus has slipped away and is sitting still and quiet with Nanak in the back room. He is not saying or doing anything, but they are clearly in some sort of companionship. After a time, Jesus comes out and gets a cup of water. He goes back in, sits down and drinks some of it before placing it between himself and Nanak. He does nothing to specifically offer the cup to Nanak who does not move for a while. But eventually, calmly and determinedly, as though the time is right, he does pick it up, and sips at it. He puts it down again and briefly smiles at Jesus.

There is a momentary stir of interest from the people in the front room who have watched this happening, but by then Nanak and Jesus have relapsed into quiet.

Jesus preaching
I am in the crowd as Jesus is teaching. Nanak is at the front and beckons me to come through and stand with him. As the teaching goes on, we find a place to sit. Then Jesus tells us a story about a big feast, of those who do not attend, and of the final order to make people come whether they want to or not. Nanak is engaged but looks a little saddened. "Jesus is sharing his weariness, his discouragement, his frustration. I feel for him and wish I could help him, but my time has not yet come, and . . . "

"And what?" I prompt.

" . . . and I think he is going to regret those last few words." How do I react to this? Defensive on behalf of Jesus, a shocked recognition that I share this perspective, and a feeling of close identification with Jesus after my own burst of irritability [an event earlier in the day on holiday]. This all produces a momentary resentment of Nanak, but then that melts away as I realize he has spoken out of concern, not judgement, and I appreciate his sharing such an intimate thought with me.

Nanak feeds the sadhus
[It seems too much "in the frame" for Jesus and me to follow Nanak throughout, but where to meet? We come across him in the marketplace where he is spending the twenty pieces of silver with which his father has

trusted him to make a profit and prove himself as a merchant. Instead he is spending it all on food for some starving holy men he has met on the way.]

I am with Jesus in the market buying a few basic needs when we become aware of excitement at some of the food stalls. It is clear that someone is spending a lot more than usual. We go over to see what is going on, and there is Nanak, spending away, with his father's servant, Bala, trying to stop him. Wheat, sugar, ghee, all in quantity. The word has gone round that he has plenty of money and is clearly intent on spending the lot. Bala gives up, standing disconsolate and anxious as the traders press round Nanak, eager for his custom. If they are expecting a soft touch, they are disappointed; he is astute in his dealings, but there are still some big sales to be made. Bala says to Jesus: "His father will be furious."

"His earthly father, perhaps," replies Jesus. Nanak hears him and they laugh together as Bala's exasperation increases.

Calling the disciples

Nanak hears Jesus preaching about the kingdom as a mustard seed, leaven, and an empty jar, and against anxiety. Nanak smiles broadly: "You have found the way."

Jesus, returning the smile, replies, "The way has found me!"

Jesus calls Simon Peter and Andrew, James and John, and Levi. Nanak and I watch, then Jesus turns to me and invites me to follow him as well. I am reluctant to leave Nanak but, knowing Jesus to be the one I must follow, I go to him.

Nanak comes with me! Later I ask, "Aren't you disappointed that Jesus didn't ask you to follow him?" He replied, "Each of us has our path. I know the time will come when I will be with my own and following the way set before me."

"But if this is not your calling why are you following Jesus now?"

"I am your companion and a friend of Jesus."

"How did you become his friend if you are not his follower?"

"We have been friends since before the world began, and not just us."

"Who else then?"

"Our friendship now is in you, and your friendship is in us." And then Nanak asks me a question: "When did that begin, do you think?"

"A couple of years ago."

He laughs kindly: "So it may seem, dear John, so it may seem."

Nanak's return

Nanak has disappeared after going into the River Bain. Three days later he reappears and proclaims, "There is no Hindu, and there is no Musselman." As people discuss his words he turns to Jesus: "Can we speak alone?" I watch them go and wonder what they are talking about. When they return Nanak is still very quiet, though his words have created a furore. I ask Jesus what they have spoken about. At first, I think I have caused offence by my curiosity, but then he says:

"Dear John, I will tell you what you can bear to hear. You remember my time of temptation in the wilderness, but there is to be another time when I shall be withdrawn from sight, returning on the third day, and we have been comparing his experience and mine."

"Which was the best?"

He doesn't answer my question, looking for a moment disappointed. Then, half to himself, he replies: "His is a beginning, mine is an end; his is a receiving, mine is a giving; his is grace, mine is sacrifice; yet there is no contrast, each complements the other."

How could I have asked such a crass question? And yet there was something about how Jesus had answered that made me glad that I had.

Exorcism

I am following with Nanak as Jesus preaches in Galilee. In one of the synagogues Jesus is challenged. He yells, "Silence! Get out of him!" A demon comes out, but instability remains in the air. There are challenges to Jesus, his challenge to the demons' authority, instability in Satan's own domain, the challenge to the religious authorities this act of power represents, the arrival of a new rule and a new kingdom (like being in the middle of a coup), and instability of identity: who will the possessed person be now? And who is Jesus?

I know Nanak is not over-impressed by works of power or with the whole deliverance business. I ask: "What do you make of this?"

"In this casting out Jesus has broadcast instability far beyond the individual and beyond the synagogue within which it was permitted to reside. There will be consequences."

"Then why did he do it?"

"For truth. He is the true one, and he is calling truth into being. But revealing is also unleashing." I see sadness on Nanak's face. "His *hukam* is becoming clear."

Lalo the carpenter

Jesus and I are among a crowd that has gathered at the house of Lalo the carpenter. We were travelling with Nanak, but, like Mardana,[144] have been staying elsewhere rather than overburden the humble craftsman. Nanak calls Jesus forward to meet Lalo, and I go too. The conversation soon shifts so that Jesus and Lalo are busy discussing the technicalities of carpentry, comparing notes on how things are done in their different cultures, as handed down by their respective fathers. Nanak is delighted by this technical conversation between friends and happy to sit quietly, despite their occasionally offering us ways into the conversation. The friendship between Jesus and Nanak is an open one which is not threatened by other friendships but enjoys them.

I am aware that outside there is some jealousy though, from the village landlord, who feels shown up because Nanak has chosen to stay with Lalo rather than him. There is also disdain among some of the onlookers, who not only despise Lalo but now place Jesus in the same lower caste of the carpenters: no Brahmin then, not even, like Nanak, a trader. But that animosity is all outside the door. For us in the house there is a warm, friendly gathering with barriers being broken down, and the technical talk between Lalo and Jesus gives it a mood of settled domesticity. Holiness is rooted, friendly, practical, without effect. Being there reminds me of my *Tarkhan* (carpenter) friends, and I feel them with me in their solidarity with Lalo.

Nanak and the *pirs*

Local holy men, Sufi *pirs*, come to Nanak as he approaches their village. They bring a cup of milk, full to the brim, implying there are enough holy men there already and Nanak is not wanted. I am about to say that Nanak is special and they should listen to him, but he gestures for me to be quiet. He calmly goes over to a jasmine bush, plucks a single leaf off a flower and gently balances it on the surface of the milk, not spilling a drop. I am moved to laughter by his clever response, not leading to antagonism but to peace and good feeling, and the tension dissipates. When he goes with them into the town, he shows such humility and grace that there is no sense of his trying to take control. I can see Jesus is impressed too. Is he perhaps thinking of the neatness and lightness of touch of this compared with his own experience of sharper conflicts and the dark uncertainties those have brought? He is smiling, but sadly. In the discourses with the *pir*s, Nanak refers to Jesus as a fellow *sant*.[145] Looking at Jesus he says: "Where a river of living water flows one leaf floats on the surface, another sinks beneath, but both are washed to the sea." I am made aware again of the mutuality Jesus and Nanak show in their friendship, neither seeking to displace the other.

The arrest of Jesus
Nanak and I are gathered with the disciples, have been with them overnight, and then the soldiers come. There is uproar as the followers of Jesus protest. Then there is Nanak, strong and bold, his knife drawn, standing there beside Jesus. A soldier makes his way towards them, spear at the ready, but Nanak moves to one side and, to show he means business, cuts the soldier's ear. For a moment the attention shifts from Jesus to Nanak, but then Jesus tells him to put the knife away. In a hushed moment, as the soldiers wait to see if Nanak will comply, Jesus touches the wounded ear and the blood ceases to flow. We are confused. If we are not to defend him then what are we to do? The soldiers take advantage of our confusion and seize Jesus, and now they start to try to grab the rest of us too. We run.

As Nanak and I draw up panting in the back streets to which we have fled, I realize I am shaking with fear and shock. They might have arrested me too; and then there was the shock of Nanak drawing his knife. I knew he carried it but had never seen him use it in earnest; he was always so skilful at diffusing anger. To see him handling himself like that in a fight confused me. And then I realized I was also shocked by Jesus' rebuke to him. I have never heard either of them speak to the other abruptly before.

We are far enough away to be safe for the moment, so we lean against the wall as we get our breath.

"You could have been killed," I say.

"I would have died for him without a moment's hesitation."

"As a friend?"

"I would defend anyone being silenced, oppressed, treated unjustly; but yes, he is my friend."

"I was shocked when he told you to stop." There, I have said it. How will he react? He looks intently at me, and then as he sees me blush, he gently looks away.

"I have known this time would come since we first met. He has his *hukam*, I have mine . . . you have yours. They may diverge for a time, but you will see, you *will* see, that there is a deeper current that brings all these different streams together. Jesus has a lonely path to follow now, the loneliest, and all of us become lonely too, his companions and friends."

As the power had drained out of Jesus and now the joy departed from Nanak, how is it that I am seeing their glory all the more? And, at this point of brutal separation, how is it that their unity is coming into sharp focus, plain, before my eyes?

Devsi tells me that the first five gurus never carried any weapon. I had made a mistake, but perhaps the spiritual rather than the historical similitude can be salvaged by remembering that "Nanak" is present in the later gurus.

Resurrection

It is early morning and Nanak and I are walking along the seashore when we come across Jesus' disciples on the beach. They have clearly been fishing and there is a very good catch in the net. We can smell that they are barbecuing some of the fish, and there next to them as they cook, right in the middle of them, is Jesus himself. We settle with them, sharing in the fish along with some bread. As time goes on Jesus has some special words for Simon Peter, and then he turns to Nanak: "My dear friend, our closeness is not defined by time or space, and those differences will not separate us, for nothing can. What the world sees as separation cannot last, and you John (Jesus turns to me) will have a part in overcoming it."

The meal eventually finishes, and we help gut and clean the rest of the fish before leaving, imitating the expert actions of the fishermen. We are loath to go, because we know this is the last time we will see Jesus in the flesh. We also know, as the apostles go one way and Nanak another, that the worldly separation Jesus spoke of is about to begin. Now I have to choose, and, according to my *hukam*, I follow Jesus, tagging along with the apostles. I am constantly looking over my shoulder and feel all the pain of parting from Nanak. Then I remember Jesus' promise that the separation will end and I take courage.

Nanak in Kartarpur
Nanak has returned to Kartarpur and retired; he has taken off his travelling clothes and put on those of a householder. I watch as the Hindu holy men question and taunt him, and one of them sneers at this new worldliness. Nanak angers them further by saying that their vaunted asceticism is turned sour by their begging. He then sits out the ensuing storm of hostility until gradually its energy is dissipated and they withdraw. His family and supporters realize that a crucial moment has passed, and now, through *langar*, through regular prayer, through generosity and hard work, through the humdrum life of the household, a new path is being established.

Although I am watching all this I am confused; I don't know what I am doing here. Since the parting of Nanak and Jesus I thought my way was to be with Jesus. I did not expect to be seeing Nanak, being accepted as a member of Nanak's household, and am not sure I should be. Still feeling uneasy I go through to *langar*. Despite my misgivings it is easy to follow the crowd, and, truth be told, I am hungry. Chapattis, lentils, spicy vegetables, rice pudding, are served swiftly and efficiently to the growing numbers. I give a nod of thanks to each of the servers. Then the man serving the rice reaches across, touches my arm, and gives the briefest of smiles as our eyes meet. I move along, no longer uneasy, and find a space to eat my twice-blessed food.

Focal points

1. Imagination is a way of entering the world of inner vision which can be an instrument of God, and it helps to make sense of experience, not being alien to reason but functioning differently.
2. It is being used here to shape a raw meditative sensation to assist in developing an appropriate theology, a theology nourished by the imagination and with an imaginative power of its own.
3. The use of imagination in this way is based on the Ignatian understanding that God is waiting to reveal himself with a revelation that should affect behaviour and attitudes.

1 0

The friendliness of God

My approach throughout the research has been rooted in practice; I wanted to let my actual engagement speak for itself rather than forcing it into any theoretical framework, something which means it now provides material for different subsequent interpretations, including those which are critical of MRP. It would be an incomplete account of the process though if I did not record, alongside the physical, emotional, and spiritual aspects of the experience, the intellectual framework that developed as it progressed. I am not claiming that this is a necessary approach to MRP, only that it is the sort of thinking that engagement in MRP can generate and it is part of the wider contention that such reflective boundary-crossing will generate theological insights. It comes towards the end as an indicator that the theory has emerged from the experience, but it is in no way privileged as a "conclusion" or the "real" meaning. The story is the thing.

The stimulus for the approach described here was the sensation of friendliness in *simran*, recognized in February 2017, and the Ignatian-based work on the imagination of friendships in September 2017. In dealings with the gatekeepers at the two gurdwaras and in my pastoral style at Beacon Church, friendship had been essential to my research and my professional practice. Those friendships increased the obligations to confidentiality, loyalty and transparency, and it meant that some relationships have been maintained after the formal research was over, though this has to be placed alongside the awkward fact that such research is inevitably using the people whose lives it is recording. Whatever the ambiguities, friendship has proved not just to be an aspect of my practice and research method, but has also developed as a theological theme.

A theology of friendship

Friendship is not universally lauded by theologians. It is contrasted unfavourably with love by some, *philia* as against *agapē*, with *philia* being seen as secondary because it is limited rather than universal, based on mutual need and subject to change. This criticism leads on to accusations that friendship can lead to injustice in civic life when a group of pals put their mutual interests before the general good, and that it is in tension with vocation where the call of God is drowned out by friendship's siren calls.[146] However, there are grounds for seeing friendship between people and between the individual and God as having great theological significance.

Most titles of Jesus—"Saviour", "Lord"—relate to imbalance of power and hierarchy, implying distance. "Friend" is an under-explored description, found in scripture where Jesus describes himself as a friend of his followers and is described by others as a friend of tax-gatherers and sinners, a title he seems to accept (Matthew 11:19; John 15:15). Barbara Kerney in her exploration of theological friendship emphasizes the range of people to whom Jesus showed friendship and claims that in his incarnation Jesus shows friendship to be the most godlike way that human beings can relate to each other.[147] Such friendship has precursors in the Hebrew Bible. Exodus 33:11 boldly states that "the LORD used to speak to Moses face to face, as one speaks to a friend."

Aelred of Rievaulx (1100–67), in his classical treatise *Spiritual Friendship*, claims that in friendship there is no hierarchy, a startling claim for an abbot to make, being near the apex of both feudal and spiritual authority, and he specifically recognizes this equality in friendship between genders.[148] Aelred affectionately exposes the characters of his perhaps fictitious proponents: timid Ivo, irascible Walter, eager-to-please Gratian, the over-stretched abbot, making respectful allowance for the shortcomings of all concerned; for true friendship is a place where the shadow side is received and accepted, and one allows one's friends to be, just the way they are.[149] Aelred made clear the need for discernment in developing a friendship, but once developed, he advocated sticking with it while there was any chance that problems might be overcome.[150]

This Christian attention to friendship is more than matched in *Sikhi*. Just the invocation of Guru Nanak's name in conversation with a Sikh, even by a complete stranger or a known rogue, is enough to establish a friendship as strong as the bonds of family.[151] Nanak was described as being accompanied during much of his twenty-three years of journeying by two boyhood friends, the musician Mardana, a Muslim, and Bala, a Hindu, friendships which crossed caste as well as religious lines. The relationship with Mardana is better attested and was particularly close. People took them for brothers because of their similar appearance, but their characters were different, Mardana's carefree and talkative nature complementing Guru Nanak's quiet thoughtfulness. The musician's continuing hunger led him into scrapes that provided light touches in the tales of their journeys, but his music was a serious contribution to Nanak's mission and to later Sikh life.[152]

God is named in the *Mool Mantra* as *Nirvair*, without enmity, and there are several names by which God is invoked in *Guru Granth Sahib Ji* which imply friendship, as well as injunctions on the subject. There are limitations on dealings with Muslims and sectarian Sikhs and there is no friendship possible with evil forces, but the Sikh way of life is one in which friendship with God and with other human beings is an important value such that union with the supreme reality leaves no room for any hostility.[153] *Sikhi*'s sense of friendship has been credited with having nurtured its development of support for human rights and equality generally.[154] It is a continuing feature of Sikh life:

> When I asked Devsi about friendship ... he told me ... about three friends of his grandfather's generation whose living together in Lahore had created such a bond that, even though their families were scattered at partition, their children have remained close down the generations, regarding each other as cousins, and that had come out of friendship.

Thomas Aquinas saw friendship with other humans (and the angels) as signs of the friendship we will all share with each other and with God in paradise. Aelred developed this, distinguishing spiritual friendship from the carnal and the worldly, which are sullied by base motives; pure friendship is the human image of God's characteristic unity, and is God's greatest gift to humankind, leading to an embrace which foreshadows the sensations of the heavenly Communion:

> ... sometimes suddenly, imperceptibly, affection melts into affection, and somehow touching the sweetness of Christ nearby, one begins to taste how dear he is and experience how sweet he is.[155]

To be attuned to Jesus as friend is to enter a creative power in which there is no question of rivalry, where Satan is banished, and where there is an extraordinary gentleness. The Spirit of God moves and remakes us while respecting our individuality. This all comes about through God's liking for us, a word which has none of the overtone of forceful intervention with which Christians have freighted the word "love", and does not imply dependence although it is sustaining.[156] In *Sikhi*, despite the issue over whether the Divine has attributes, the devout can still have friendship with God: "I have befriended only the one God: I love only the one God. Yea, the one alone is my constant companion and friend", and he can be experienced as the best companion, closer than family.[157] This friendship is strengthened and made effectual in its turn by friendship with those who are themselves under the influence of the gurus.[158]

There are problems with the idea of a friendship with God, and the Lord's friendly meeting with Moses is set in a context that seems to contradict that domesticated image, a context in which the terrifying glory of God is repeatedly emphasized. Claims of friendship may be felt to diminish the authority of God, but, as with Aelred's monastic authority, divine authority is bracketed rather than denied in the context of friendship. This realization helped with the issue of submission that had troubled me in discussions at one of the focus groups. Friendship may give the opportunity to flout the authority of a superior, but it takes away the desire. Paul addressed a similar issue over the possibility of taking advantage of grace, demonstrating that this was not a problem specific to the friendship model but to any approach that rested on a relationship with a generous and merciful God (Romans 6:14 f.).

I have so far dwelt exclusively on the friendly aspects of Jesus and Guru Nanak as indicated in scripture and in the *janam-sakhi* and *Guru Granth Sahib Ji*, but acknowledge that more divisive and judgemental presentations of Jesus' lordship and messages from the writings of the gurus can be found as well. I recognize this shadow side, but, as people do with unpalatable aspects of their friends, I choose to set these factors in a wider more amiable context and so do not dwell on them. Recognizing the existence of this difficult side is not incompatible with friendship since strangely we love people for their apparent shortcomings as much as for their virtues. In any case, Christianity and *Sikhi* both insist that devotees should regard with love the all-powerful maker and sustainer of mortal existence despite the terrors and evils of that existence. The resilience experienced in friendship may provide a better way of dealing with this challenging expectation than anything offered by the suspect vindications of systematic theodicy.[159]

A further twist brings one last problem into sight: if coping with one another's shortcomings is one of the building-blocks of friendship then divine perfection is as much an obstacle to friendship as any shadow side. However, Jesus, being our friend, not only covers our shortcomings, but he also invites us to "cover" (without needing to reject) his outstanding goodness, a goodness which would otherwise unbalance the equality of true friendship. When a rich young man asked: "'Good Teacher, what must I do to inherit eternal life?' Jesus said to him, 'Why do you call me good? No one is good but God alone" (Mark 10:17–18).

Interreligious friendship

These features of divine friendship can be brought into the interreligious context: prevention of rivalry, loss of hierarchy, acceptance of a shadow side, and covering of perfection, and they throw into disarray the competitive and judgemental aspects followers adopt on behalf of their religions, and with them the desire to displace their rivals.

As a general statement difference does not prevent friendship. Research has shown that friendship is understood in similar ways in different cultures; experience of cross-cultural friendship reduces the need for similarity of lives and experiences in forming further friendships; and friendships can grow despite difference through shared activity including ritual.[160] Difference is not necessarily an obstacle to friendship in Christian scripture and in the example of Jesus, and deep friendship moves us towards the integration with all reality that is key to Sikh spirituality.[161] Devsi told me that his most long-standing friends in Britain are a Muslim and a Hindu.

What models for interreligious friendship do we see in Jesus and Guru Nanak? There was hostility between Jesus and some of the authorities of his own faith, Judaism (though even there Jesus begins in mutuality and discussion—Luke 2:41–51), but that relationship is an unnecessarily negative model for imagining Jesus' dealings with Nanak. These second-order upholders of the institution have an important religious role, but it is different from that of religious founders such as Jesus and Nanak. Jesus had dealings with only one holy-man religious founder, John the Baptist, and Jesus' reaction is one of a submission that seemed to signify his own commitment to John's cause, to the embarrassment of later Christian writers.[162] Although John's apocalyptic style was different from Nanak's, his actual message to tax collectors and soldiers to work honestly and his challenge to religiosity (Luke 3:7–14) are as close to Nanak's message as to Jesus. It is harder to distinguish between holy men and women and institutional religious functionaries in Nanak's milieu, and he had his confrontations with the latter, e.g. in his refusal of the thread ceremony, *yagnopavitam*. However, his dealings with the *pirs* of Multan demonstrated his capacity for turning religious confrontation into friendship.

Interreligious friendship can be a goal in itself but is also an invitation to learning, including self-understanding. Friendship is seen as an aim and natural outcome of most sustained dialogue rather than just an enabler. A form of friendship is sometimes advocated in Christian evangelism, though some evangelists are uneasy about using friendship as a tool, and such behaviour has given rise to Sikh distrust.[163] Interreligious friendship can be a matter of Christian vocation, as for Thomas Merton, whose original doctrinal boundaries were challenged by a "vocation of unity"; and it can have a sacramental aspect as an experience of grace and a foretaste of eternal joy.[164] For Sikhs, it can be seen as a particularly powerful aspect of that transformation by integration which is associated with all friendships.

Brian McLaren explores interreligious friendship through his own extensive imaginative exercise in which he asks if Jesus, Muhammad, Moses, the Buddha—and he draws in Guru Nanak and others—would compete when they met, or would reach out their hands in friendship and embrace, being drawn towards one another as friends, allies, and collaborators, and McLaren recognizes that such a possibility makes claims on their followers. He seeks a religious identity that is both strong and benevolent, one (for a Christian) both rooted in Christ and open, not as factors in tension but pointing in the same direction, because Christ is himself open and generous.[165] The tension between faiths, regarded by some as inevitable, almost a badge of faith, should be dissipated in the warmth of our religious leaders and our God, removed rather than caused by faith.

Such imaginary work may seem a tenuous basis for theology in that Nanak and Jesus never actually met. However, theology gives room for speculation outside history, as Christian scripture indicates that the communion of saints is neither bound by time nor confined to Christians. Jesus said: "Your ancestor Abraham rejoiced that he would see my day; he saw it and was glad" (John 8:56). I asked Devsi if Guru Nanak is still in existence, or whether the attainment of *mukti*, release from reincarnation, involved loss of personhood. He replied that Sikh teaching has it that Nanak is alive in the sequence of the gurus including *Guru Granth Sahib Ji*, in the *sangat*, and in the souls of individual worshippers. This assured me that the friendliness I experienced in *simran* could be related to the personhood of Nanak being present within me alongside Jesus. As by the Spirit Christ dwells in my heart through faith (Ephesians 3:17), his meeting with Nanak was not just something for a theoretical cosmic realm but had a venue much closer to home. Mark Stobert, my spiritual director, had once invited me to explore being an incarnation of both Christ and the Guru together, and I had wondered at that, responding, "If I am inhabiting Jesus and the Guru [or they me] the conflict goes, I become a point where they meet." McLaren's imaginative exercise and my own were not floating free despite their lack of historical base but were anchored in formal theology and personal spirituality alike.

It is acknowledged that the warmth of regard between religions described here is not universal; friendship is discriminatory by nature. Jesus is described as having a special relationship with one disciple described as *agapētós*, "beloved", a word that suggests a "spontaneous and irrational" aspect to the relationship.[166] Ethical discernment is also essential. Some religious manifestations are cruel, dangerous, and destructive; they may be approached with initial friendliness but as their nature becomes apparent that friendship cannot be developed, a judgement to be reached with regret. Furthermore, friendship requires reciprocity: it cannot be imposed on one party by another, and not all religions present themselves to all others as friendly. Where relations between religions fall foul of these restraints there may still be friendships between individuals of different faiths; however, their religions are not aspects of that friendship but mark a difference that has to be somehow worked round by the friends.

Amicism

Friendships may have an inevitable limit to their scope, but *friendliness* is a disposition towards the world, and I thought of my experience in the gurdwara as one of that more general friendliness. Friendliness is taken to be an individual's or community's approach to the world marked by openness, thinking well of others, interest in them, and vulnerability to rebuff or exploitation. The relationship between friendship and friendliness is subtle. Friendliness without any actual friendships would be either superficial or tragic; friendships without more general friendliness is the stuff of divisive cliques. An attitude of friendliness is not reserved for friends themselves, indeed it is more clearly demonstrated to strangers or mere acquaintances. Friendliness may, like friendship, be found to be inappropriate; heart-felt friendliness is vulnerable to rejection and exploitation, an aspect of its generous and potentially sacrificial nature. It does not prevent or do away with the need for discernment, which is true within religions and in secular settings as much as between religions. But it does bring an initial amiability and hope to all potential relationships. If theologians and interreligious scholars have not considered friendship as much as they might, there has been even less attention paid to the general attitude of friendliness, this positive attitude. The warmth I was experiencing during meditation in the gurdwara linked back to my experience of Jesus' friendliness in the vision, to the friendliness with which I was treated in church and gurdwara, and to stories of Nanak's own friendliness. The initial sensation was the warmth of being accepted, welcome, enjoyed, and invited to respond, and it felt cosmic in range with no question of preference or privilege.

Bearing this in mind I am proposing an approach which sees friendliness as the appropriate initial attitude between religions themselves, an approach which I am calling amicism. I am therefore moving beyond interreligious relationalism, which acknowledges the pre-existing cultural, theological, and historical entanglements of religions, and going on to suggest how those relationships should develop. "Amicism" does not appear in standard dictionaries[167] but has been used in management consultancy, where it is related to a business structure which is affected (and distorted) by friendship networks. It is seen negatively as something that blocks social mobility, but researchers have had to acknowledge that despite its drawbacks amicism is hard to replace in providing the empathy necessary for an effective workplace.[168] I use a more generic and less critical definition of amicism as "the promotion of an initial friendliness as appropriate to interreligious and other relationships and staying open to the possibility of friendships growing in those relationships".

If Jesus Christ is seen as friendly, this friendliness needs to be demonstrated in all aspects of Christian theology and mission, and a similar conclusion can be reached for followers of the friendly Guru Nanak. My focus is primarily on relations between religions as such, not relationships between individuals, communities, or institutions, though it should assist with those. Amicism should arise in any religious context where the believer holds a personification (historical, mythical, or philosophical) of her or his religion to be friendly, and if this is the position of a wider tradition such friendliness should influence structural and theoretical aspects of that community's relationships.

This is not a cost-free approach. I have remarked that to be friendly opens us up to rebuff and to exploitation as the offered friendship is rejected or abused. It is also to lay aside a significant tool in establishing and defending religious—and often therefore cultural and political—identity. Identity strategies for individuals include something called "betterment distancing", the rejection or breach of friendships that would damage their identity or image, that would drag them down or show them up.[169] This is not just a strategy for individuals; whole communities also identify themselves by who they are not, and for religious communities that seems a particularly powerful agenda. It is one that amicism cuts across, generating a vulnerability not only to particular slights, but also at this more existential level of identity maintenance. Fortunately religions have other more positive means to identify themselves, by describing what they admire and wish to emulate from their neighbours, and acknowledging the network of mutualities in which they are already bound.

This adjustment of priorities is recognizable in David Cheetham's plea for meeting between people of different religions at points of depth not claimed by theological meanings, where the inner dynamic of the person is able to embrace the deep experiences of a person of another religion, perhaps in relation to creation and beauty in a spirit of God-given play.[170] Do theological issues really have to be set aside as Cheetham advises for this deep-rooted friendliness to be expressed, or can it be expressed within that theology?

Theological problems rarely arise directly from the relationship between the faith communities on the ground, a matter for social and political skill, or from the ultimate theological issues of the nature of divinity, where descriptions are sufficiently tentative and paradoxical to allow some accommodation. It is in the middle ground, historical understanding and the status of leaders, founders or scriptures, where the difficulties are sharpest, and it is there that two suggestions from Cheetham offer ways of dynamic meeting in which amicist theology could be fruitful. First, he describes having a "multi-self" as both healthy and an aspect of the image of God within us all. It is a "relating self" marked by "an inner skilfulness or lightness of spirit that is characterized by joy," carrying "others' experiences, dreams and sufferings".[171] The second is that he describes his book *Ways of Meeting and the Theology of Religions* as "an exploration in imagination", seeking "to develop imaginative or even playful ways of engaging".[172] In the face of the gritty questions of competitive religious identity, this image of the divine—and therefore of Jesus and Nanak—as relational, light of spirit, and joyful changes the tone of meeting. It brings into imaginative focus the friendship between faith founders, a friendship that binds together those who follow them rather than letting their respective loyalties drive them apart. Where a person's multi-self provides the setting for such a meeting this can be regarded as gain rather than weakness, a point of integration and a source of new insight.

Amicism—a summary

If Jesus is friendly, and he and other religious leaders can be thought of as friends as in McLaren's imagining, then the relation between their religions should reflect that. Amicism therefore proposes an initial approach of *friendliness* to all religions, a friendliness that is open, joyful, peaceable, vulnerable, and discerning. Amicism also encourages specific *friendships*, albeit with discernment and inevitable preferences. In these friendships there is no regard for status, so competition between followers is otiose. Such friends are capable of criticism but prefer to praise, and are pleased by the other's success. MRP is one of many ways in which amicism can be pursued, a way of expressing divine friendliness and developing divine friendships in the interreligious context.

Friendliness is a personal or communal attitude, but amicism sets a theological pattern, modelled for Christians on the relationship between earth and heaven (Psalm 85:10–11)[173], to be advocated between religions and communities, and more widely in civic and international life. Birmingham Council of Christian Churches launched a related campaign in May 2018, *Permission to Smile*, but if good-natured approaches like this are to bring significant changes in social attitudes they need to lead to the deeper engagement proposed here, changes where our own identities—including religious identities—are allowed to become more open. The employment of amicism as an imaginative theological exercise encourages that openness, allowing relations to move beyond superficial bonhomie and objectivized mutual discussion to shared, lived exploration. This does not mean that everything discovered will be acceptable or that discernment is no longer required, but it does mean that even significant difference need not prevent religious engagement at the deepest level, and that such engagement is not in itself a betrayal of the first religion. Taking the liberty to do this would deepen personal and institutional interreligious relationships immeasurably, developing a more benign theology and releasing a spiritual energy with social consequences that could dissipate the anxiety that often seems to bedevil the interreligious agenda.

Focal points

1. Divine friendliness had developed from my experience throughout the research and particularly in *simran* as a theological as well as an imaginative theme.
2. Features of divine friendship that can be brought into the interreligious context include: prevention of rivalry, loss of hierarchy, acceptance of a shadow side, and covering of perfection. They throw into disarray the competitive and judgemental aspects followers adopt on behalf of their respective revelations of divinity.
3. The tension between faiths, regarded by some as inevitable, almost a badge of faith, should be dissipated in the warmth of our religious leaders and our God, removed rather than caused by faith.
4. One locus of interreligious friendship is within the spirit of the individual practitioner of MRP.
5. Friendship must always be a matter of discernment and is limited in scope.
6. Friendliness, however, is an attitude towards the world, and divine friendliness is cosmic in range. It brings an initial amiability and hope to all potential relationships, is generous and potentially sacrificial. This openheartedness makes it vulnerable to rejection and exploitation, but it is capable of restoration.
7. Friendliness is attributed by their traditions to both Jesus Christ and Guru Nanak.

8. "Amicism" is proposed as an approach to interreligious relations marked by this friendliness, an approach which makes betterment distancing an inappropriate means of protecting religious identity. The identity, thus softened, becomes a relating identity, as for example in MRP, marked by lightness and joy.
9. This attitude, if nurtured in interreligious relations, has a benign role to play in wider community, civic, and international life.

11

Taking stock

This story has not yet ended, so to speak of a conclusion is premature, nor is this ever-changing exercise in experience and reflection capable of summary. However, the ending of the book is an occasion for looking over the research and trying to identify what has come to light.

No discernible harm was done by the research. The ethical issues of confidentiality, fair representation, and researcher safety, considered carefully beforehand, were dealt with satisfactorily (provisional on the consequences of publication), as shown by the responses of those involved when they read the research report, and by my own continuing wellbeing.

I maintain a loyalty to Christianity which I defended on the one occasion when it was questioned, and continue to be of good standing with church authorities. The research reveals limits to my engagement with *Sikhi*, some of which were practical and social, connected with time available, language difference, or gurdwara organization. Others, preventing me becoming *Amritdhari* or *Sahajdhari*, arose out of my continuing commitment to Christianity. Some nonetheless saw me as a Sikh, and on occasion I defined myself as a Sikh-Christian or a *Nanak panthi* without being contradicted.

New and useful insights into interreligious relations were opened up by this careful description of and reflection on embarking on a pattern of MRP, in particular:

1. It makes clear the fluidity and complexity of religious belonging in its personal, bodily, communal, and formal aspects from the point of view of someone initiating MRP. It challenges the rigidity of religious belonging that political and administrative bodies assume and religious institutions advocate, a rigidity that feeds

identity politics and discrimination. This relates to developing discussions in religious studies of the complexity of belonging.[174]
2. It has contributed to professional understanding by exposing that DIFAs routinely experience subjective participation in the worship of non-Christian faiths but have no opportunity to reflect on this in a structured way and are anxious about the reaction of the wider church. It encourages them to be more reflective but bolder in such crossing of borders, and the Church to be more ready to attend to what they find.
3. It has contributed to theology of religions by proposing that MRP and other border-crossing is best set in the context of amicism, an approach of religious friendliness marked by openness, joy, vulnerability, and discernment, and leading to specific interreligious friendships. Consideration of amicism arose from the author's sensation of divine friendliness while meditating in the gurdwara, illustrating the theoretical stimulus found in the experience of boundary-crossing.
4. It has contributed to practical theology (see the appendix below) by offering a reflective narrative on interreligious engagement, and bringing together action, reflection—including imagination—and theological theory. It has demonstrated the opportunities opened up by practical theology's creative approach to research.
5. It points to the need for further work in developing understandings of religions that regard identity-marking strategies with suspicion, bearing in mind political, social, institutional, and market drivers; and recognizing that identity-making has an energy of its own, not necessarily evil, but with a different agenda from the religions to which it attaches itself. *Sikhi* offers a way into this issue through Guru Nanak's declaration, "There is no Hindu, there is no Muslim."

In making my findings public I am inviting readers and the wider audience who hear about this research to engage in re-imagining the world, with the boundaries between religions no longer regarded as defended borders marked by fear, aggression, and evasion, but as playing-fields of mutual delight, affection, and truthfulness.

Coda

It is March 2020. I have been diligent in attending weekly *seva* in Birmingham, and have kept up a monthly attendance at GKN until the beginning of the lockdown due to the COVID-19 pandemic. I had settled into that pattern and no longer felt the sense of withdrawal experienced when I first retired. In August 2018, I attended a *simran* (Sikh meditation) camp for the first time at the invitation of someone I had interviewed, and was introduced to "Tenth Gate" mysticism, the spiritual gate which can be opened alongside the nine physical portals;[175] and in September I took my wife with a member of our local church to GKN gurdwara on a visit, something they both much appreciated. This was my wife's first visit. In 2019, I was invited onto the committee of GKN's community association, a body which is seeking to develop community use in the building. These all feel like ways in which I am becoming more integrated with *Sikhi* and with the gurdwara over the years, although I don't really understand the relationship between the association and the gurdwara's own management committee (something in which I suspect I am not alone). Until lockdown I occasionally led worship at my parish church and others, as well as at Birmingham Cathedral some early mornings.

It has occurred to me that all this storytelling about divine friendliness is in essence doctrinal; the hard-wired human instinct for meaning-making has brought me back to an aspect of Christianity by which I had once felt oppressed. Realizing this is leading me to wonder what other doctrines can be experienced as imaginative, joyful, and experience-related invitations, rather than the formulaic, disciplinary, and experience-denying blinkers they had for a while become for me. This more open attitude also colours my continuing exploration of the highways and byways of Sikh tradition. And so, with renewed curiosity and enthusiasm, my own story of multiple religious participation and reflection continues . . .

APPENDIX

Under the bonnet

This is for those who would like to know more about the research process itself, the methods and principles followed, and how I went about writing it up. Before going into detail it should be said that at its heart there was a simple idea involving a period of worshipping with communities of two different religions, engaging with both as fully as possible, and reflecting on the experience without specific expectations except for any researcher's general hope that it would be worthwhile.

Method

The fieldwork ran from September 2015 to July 2017, with preparatory visits and a prolonged sequel still continuing in 2020, and was centred on weekly participation in worship at both church and gurdwara. Looking at my experience from the point of view of a researching observer inevitably had a distancing effect in both venues, as did the initial cultural, theological, and linguistic distance in my experience of Sikh worship. However, I joined in the worship wholeheartedly in gurdwara as well as church, a change from my previous stance in other-faith settings of merely allowing myself to enter into worship if that happened naturally. I had decided to withdraw to observer mode if anything about Sikh worship made me uncomfortable, but that never happened. My initial choice to engage with Sikhs through attendance at a gurdwara rather than in other ways was unreflected, the reflex of a religious professional, although it did lead to other kinds of engagement, most notably in feeding the homeless. There were advantages to focussing on meetings in the gurdwara: rituals are the most challenging aspects of a community, with power to attract and repel; they are identity markers; and they can enable contacts at emotional and spiritual levels.

I chose to make my engagement with the gurdwara weekly because this was manageable within my work timetable and might be possible for other DIFAs; it roughly paralleled my church attendance; and I had my bishop's permission for weekly engagement. Weekly or more frequent attendance at the gurdwara was found in a 2013 survey to be the practice of 39 per cent of Sikhs, so this was a reasonable attendance for me to undertake, though slightly less or slightly more regular attendance may have had significantly different effects.[176] I sought to balance Christian and Sikh worship, but MRP usually involves engagement with a first, more rooted, religion while drawing on a second, and this asymmetry in engagement, weighted towards Christianity, was unavoidable.

I considered taking notes during my visits but was aware of the tension between doing this and immersion in the experience, so settled for recording my experience of church about half an hour after leaving (after my drive to the gurdwara) and immediately after leaving the gurdwara, the promptness reducing the risk of inaccurate and biased recall. On a few occasions I had to alter that pattern because of following engagements, but made good as soon as possible. I would type the notes up later in the week. There were eighty-eight visits to church recorded and eighty-three to gurdwaras.[177] The notes were traditional field notes recording what was going on around me, but I also recorded my own activity and feelings, included any errors, and noted my reflections at that time. I took some photographs, taking care not to photograph people without permission, and collected artefacts, mainly leaflets, booklets, and free newspapers from the gurdwara, but also Sikh outreach material from other sources, and a number of gifts: a Sikh wall calendar, a copy of the gurdwara constitution, and the *siropa* and engraved plate which were presented to me. It was not possible to identify church-related items as "artefacts" as they were the usual acquisitions made in the course of my work.

I kept a journal in which to record my research process, professional, personal, and theological activity, mood, and comments. It was written longhand, indicating that it was personal and confidential, though I did use material from it in some shared reflections and in this book. It could have provided a therapeutic space to work through things that were troubling me, but was more usually somewhere to note otherwise fleeting ideas and emotions for further reflection.

For an external view of how MRP was affecting my religious identity I arranged to meet quarterly with two contacts I called my "collocutors", one Christian (five meetings[178]) and one Sikh (eight meetings). Each was invited to interview me and comment on how much they considered me Christian or Sikh. My Christian collocutors were Warren Bardesley, a Methodist minister with considerable experience in interfaith matters, and then Deb Dyson, an Anglican priest who had conducted my ministerial development review for the diocese and had shown an interest in this area. They were confident throughout that I remained a Christian. The Sikh, Bhajan Singh Devsi, is *Amritdhari*. He is vice-chair of Wolverhampton Interfaith, and chair of BME United Co., a Wolverhampton social enterprise, and by the end of the research period he was happy to describe me as a Sikh. Our meetings included those assessments, but Devsi also schooled me in *Sikhi*. Meetings with them were recorded with near-transcripts taken, and lasted about an hour. I also met with my spiritual director, Mark Stobert, a member of the British Council of Counsellors and Psychotherapists and fellow practitioner in practical theology. We met twelve times at roughly six-weekly intervals, for a timed hour, fully noted but not transcribed. This attention to my wellbeing helped meet one of the university's ethical requirements, and the meetings enabled consideration of different spiritual models for my experience.

As well as examining my own experience, I was trying to set it in a wider context, which included reading about academic, social, and religious interest in MRP. I also conducted eighteen interviews with people having experience across the Christian/Sikh boundary through living in mixed families, conversion, or other cross-religious activity. There were two focus groups, each about an hour and a half long with different groups of four interfaith colleagues, and one with parochial clergy colleagues which lasted just under an hour. From recordings of interviews and focus groups I typed up near-transcripts, tidying grammar and leaving occasional gaps where we had wandered away from the subject. I was also deepening my reading about *Sikhi*, although I chose to delay that for a while to leave room for my initial experiences to speak for themselves. It was therefore nine months into my visits that I renewed my reading about *Sikhi*, but then I read as widely as I could, from books, articles, and on websites, taking notes as I went along.

Journal, fieldwork, collocutions, guided reflections, interviews, focus groups, and notes from reading were drawn on for a reflective piece before each meeting with my academic adviser, Stephen Pattison, placing these meetings at the apex of reflection, though with a cyclical aspect because outcomes from that would be fed back into other points of reflection. These meetings took an unusual form, with my adviser being restrained in sharing his own reactions, allowing room for my own reflective process. What might have felt an unsettling lack of engagement was fully discussed, and I appreciated the space it gave to our meetings. I also developed the monthly self-questionnaire concerning my religious identity and reactions to the research, which I deliberately did not review until the research had finished.

All the while I was trying to interpret what I was writing, something which included computer-assisted analysis of the data I had amassed, particularly helpful in detecting themes that might have been overlooked. I also considered the significance of the research with others, including selected readers. In my agreements with church and gurdwara I had committed myself to discuss matters as we proceeded and to report back to them after twelve months, which I did. I also took up the offer to write in a Punjabi newspaper in order to relate to the wider Sikh community, and a member from the gurdwara and one from church both read a late draft of the research report with the invitation to comment, and to share it with fellow worshippers as they saw fit. Three colleagues, the Sikh and Christian collocutors, my spiritual director, a family member, and a couple of academic readers were also invited to read and comment, to improve the end product but also to express my accountability to them, acknowledging it was their story as well as mine. The representatives of the two communities with which I was engaged accepted what I had said about them, and those who had accompanied me as collocutors were satisfied with the representations of our discussions, except that Devsi made three amendments which I have recorded.[179] There were suggestions for further reading, most of which I took, and there were many individual suggestions for improvement or extension, to all of which I responded, accepting many. My academic adviser commented that making my mistakes public gave rise to a sense of embarrassment for me. I left the reports of my mistakes, but adjusted the self-deprecating style and introduced the bishop's letter of praise to give a more balanced view of my competence.

To sum up, my method was: to participate in Christian and Sikh worship; write about that experience with initial reflections in field notes; reflect on my broader experience in a journal; investigate it with a monthly self-questionnaire; contextualize the experience by reading, interviews, and focus groups, discussion with collocutors and guided reflection; take academic advice as it developed; use computer analysis of the material; and then share and test it with others involved or interested.

Principles of this research

My aim was to encourage deepening religious relationships and so advance social and religious harmony. There is no ethical code for DIFAs per se, but there are guidelines for all clergy in the Church of England, which state that: "The clergy should promote reconciliation in the Church and in the world wherever there are divisions, including those which exist between people of different faiths."[180] Ministers who find that they are no longer in good conscience able to believe, hold or teach the Christian faith as the Church of England has received it are to seek advice and help in deciding whether to continue in public ministry, but that was not the starting point of my research nor did it arise in any acute form.[181]

The university's ethics process was also useful in clarifying my responsibilities. There was concern for myself, as researchers have identified some psychological risks in fieldwork such as this which relates to personal identity: risks of anger, distress, and vulnerability.[182] The stories of many other people and communities were also involved, and this clearly brought with it a responsibility to them too. I allowed interviewees and participants in focus groups to edit my notes of meetings, and sought permission to quote from them, inviting them to return any amendments or conditions, and I received a number of cautious responses:

> I am happy for you to use the material carefully, i.e. there may be some areas of sensitivity where quoting me verbatim may not be helpful. I'm sure you'll recognize such places . . .
>
> I would like the use of the Sikh scriptures in our church to be anonymous.
>
> You can use the notes, but I do need complete anonymity please— no indication who comments are from [. . .] please.

There were also amendments protecting the identities of third parties or moderating blunt language. These caveats demonstrated the sensitivity of Christians engaging in the worship of other religions, and of issues surrounding Sikh identity, and I complied with them all.

As to the fieldwork, I had permission to research from the governing councils of the locations but not from individuals. I followed the general guidelines of informed consent: prohibition of deception, privacy, confidentiality, and accuracy, along with the golden thread of "do no harm". I felt I could not identify individuals in those settings, something which has inevitably reduced characterization in the narrative. Even showing a late draft to representatives of the two communities did not absolve me from the responsibility to make these decisions, as I felt (unlike with the texts of the interviews) a responsibility to retain editorial control of my own description of events and impressions. This had to be a matter for my own judgement, with the liberty and the responsibility that entailed.

I used myself as the focus of research because of the access required to understand the effect of MRP as deeply as possible emotionally, spiritually, and practically, and because of the psychological risks referred to above. These made it impractical and unethical to ask someone else to do it for me despite the possible benefits for them of enhanced religious understanding and wider sympathies. Exploring one's own experience has a recognized academic context in the practice of autoethnography, which researches "the interplay of introspective, personally engaged selves and cultural beliefs, practices, systems, and experiences".[183] Among its features the following relate to this research: observing as an ethnographer and describing as a storyteller; and working the territory between the orienting and disorienting story.[184] The particular experience of an observer is important where it challenges and critiques dominant social models, accepting personal vulnerability in order to understand and change society.[185] Autoethnography is more than a method, having its own principles which include: respect for qualitative research, i.e. for research with a local, concrete, embodied starting point from which to question generalizations; concern for the political, particularly with regard to identity-related issues; and an appreciation of the significance of narrative, of the emotions and of the body.[186]

My own research was in accordance with all these aspects. On the other hand, it was unusual autoethnographic research in that the setting was contrived, at least in part, and it challenged my identity rather than engaging with a pre-established identity or life experience.

The genre of autoethnography is open to challenge. Its egocentric flavour (all those "I"s and "me"s) sits ill with the cool and passive language of traditional research, but self-negation is becoming less *de rigeur*, with researchers in many disciplines and contexts now overtly appearing in their own research. More worryingly, any egocentricity jars with the turning away from ego associated with *Sikhi*; it seems *manmukh* rather than *gurmukh*. By giving some indication of my mistakes and failings I hope I have avoided a boastful narrative, but confession is as self-centred as self-promotion, as is this current display of defensiveness. What the book does show, however, is the plasticity of my identity that has been put into play, and the book also suggests that under the aspect of friendship, unselfconsciousness can gently develop. Reflective writing may seem self-obsessed, but it can be a way of liberation, recognizing and challenging taken-for-granted identity markers, and allowing writers to look aslant at their own lives. I hope one outcome of the research and this book is that readers will be encouraged to sit more loosely to their own identity, especially their religious identity, yielding it to the living God.

Autoethnography is also vulnerable to the charge of being too personal to provide public truth. A defence to this charge is that individuals are products of their environment and so can be articulating the experience of a cultural group, or even of humanity as a whole. This latter possibility has been criticized as claiming a universalism for the views of a Western, male sub-culture, and as self-absorbed therapy, but the hope in my case is that deliberate engagement with another culture, even if inevitably filtered through my own context, will broaden horizons and reduce cultural self-centredness. In my own case what I have written is "public truth" to the extent that members of the gurdwara and church involved and other partners have read it through and recognize it as accurate, and it engages with a form of religious activity, MRP, which is clearly observable in the public sphere. As with any research readers are invited to consider their own experience or related research to make their own assessment of this account, and in this case to construe it for theological as well as academic truthfulness.

I was committed to an approach that would attend to lived experience, but would also be theological. A welcoming context for this approach is found in the discipline of practical theology through its engagement with professional development and particularly with reflective writing. Practical theology is a "confessional science of the human spirit".[187] It connects theological tradition with human experience and behaviour, not just as commentary but as a means of transformative engagement. There is a welcome recognition that theology is shaped by culture, contemporary thought forms and personal experience alongside scripture and tradition.[188]

When I started to engage with the academic discipline of practical theology, it was still a moot point as to whether it could relate to interreligious and non-Christian religious exploration or whether it was inherently Christian, and relevant issues of method had not been addressed. In 2010 it was said that other religions could only be approached on Christian terms, and a major survey of the discipline in 2012 overlooked non-Christian religions beyond describing them as an area where there is room for development.[189] Some writers were addressing this area, however, and interreligious matters are now sitting more easily within the discipline, exemplified by Ray Gaston's *Faith, Hope and Love* and the work of two Muslim practical theologians, Nazila Isandarova and Asgar Rajput. This book continues the trend of practical theology towards working with non-Christian sources and approaches but how this is to be done requires further exploration. Here I have sought to apply two different theologies, Christian and Sikh, doing so with the presumption of a reader versed in Christianity but not *Sikhi*. This reflects my own particular position, but also mirrors the current state of the discipline. It may be a useful model for other authors, or lead to further discussion within the discipline as to its appropriateness.

This research had a professional as well as a theological context, but it did not have the pragmatism of some work-based learning. The hoped-for outcome was a new understanding which might have any number of consequences rather than the establishment of a specific change in practice; it was investigating the application of underlying values, seeking a deepened, more comprehensive and more intimate relationship between Christianity and *Sikhi*, as well as looking to develop understanding and skills useful in other relationships across religions. It was intended as an "appreciative enquiry" where the outcome of the research should be to encourage those being researched, gurdwara and church, with any risk being borne by the researcher who was revealing his incompetence and exposing uncertainties and vulnerabilities.

In summary, this autoethnographic research was to be ethical, theological, and professional.

The narrative approach

In describing my engagement in MRP, I told the story and was fortunate to find in practical theology an academic discipline in which narrative is taken seriously. The narrative turn in theology recognizes the healing potential of truth-telling in this way rather than by propositions, with the reader entering into the story and so being changed by it, and it is my desire to change and challenge but also to heal.[190] Narrative is also closely related to the issue of Christian identity, personal and communal, with testimony and church and denominational history having an important role. Finally, narrative allows for the expression of emotional reaction and the description of non-rational experiences, which are important data for this research.

There are some problems with the narrative approach of which the reader needs to be aware. First, in its apparent artlessness, it can seem to be an unmediated report, whereas it is the result of much editing and rearrangement. I have used less than a fifth of the material that was gathered. The reader is entitled to wonder why I have shaped the material in this way and not in any other, but might be helped in this by the indications I have given about my motives, religion, ethnicity and race, nationality, gender, sexuality, age, profession, and class.

Second, "story" is itself seductive, with its drive towards a coherent plot, a dramatic shaping to the unfolding of events. I have tried to resist this, leaving some aspects hanging in the air and demonstrating some confusion, and the "conclusion" is deliberately subverted by indications of continuing engagement. The positive plotline is also put in tension by the bathos of my mistakes. These are, in short, indications of the irregularities of human experience which theologians, like preachers, are often overquick to disguise with imposed coherence and bogus happy endings.[191] Even when these problems are taken into account it remains important that stories, the lifeblood of human interaction, are told, especially in areas where more conceptual approaches are making heavy weather.

One final note on storytelling. Not only the experience but the writing itself has changed me. Writing has given me direction at times of stress and has kept me alert to the possibility of change at times when things seemed static, and the creativity required has renewed my hope that our different religious engagements have the potential to draw humanity together rather than tearing us apart.

Focal points

1. At heart, the research involved worshipping with communities of two different religions and reflecting on the experience without specific expectations.
2. I had a duty of care towards the communities and individuals involved in my research and to myself, an aim to improve—or at least not to harm—interreligious relations, as well as a duty to the truth.
3. The research was a piece of practical theology, connecting theological tradition with human experience and behaviour as a

means of transformative engagement. Its context was Christian, but it also sought to indicate Sikh understandings.
4. It was work-based research by reflective practice and looked to develop understanding and skills useful in other relationships across religions. It was intended as appreciative enquiry where the research should encourage those being researched.
5. Although presented as narrative, the writer has tried to resist the contrivances of plot and suggest the underlying untidy reality. He has also tried to be open about his own attitudes, but acknowledges that this is a highly edited account.
6. Narrative is notable for its power to engage, challenge, and heal. It is closely related to the issue of Christian identity through testimony and history, and it gives room for the expression of meaningful emotions and non-rational experiences.
7. The creativity required in storytelling is a fitting medium for the advocacy of a more creative approach to interreligious relations generally and MRP in particular.

Bibliography

Adams, T. E., Jones, S. H., and Ellis, C., *Autoethnography: Understanding Qualitative Research* (Oxford: Oxford University Press, 2015).

Aelred of Rievaulx, *Spiritual Friendship*, tr. L. C. Braceland (Collegeville, MN: Liturgical Press, 2010).

Appiah, K. A., *Reith Lectures 2016. Mistaken Identities: Creed, Country, Color* [sic]*, Culture. Lecture 1: Creed*, available at <https://www.bbc.co.uk/programmes/b07z43ds>, accessed 26 August 2020.

Austin, M., *Explorations in Art, Theology and Imagination* (London: Routledge, Taylor and Francis Group, 2014).

von Balthasar, H. U., *Who is a Christian?*, 5th edn, tr. F. Davidson (San Francisco, CA: Ignatius Press, 2010).

Barnett, J. R., *What New and Useful Understanding of Interreligious Relations can be Opened Up by Engaging in Regular Sikh Worship while Continuing as a Practising Christian?*, DPT Thesis, University of Birmingham, 2019, available at <https://etheses.bham.ac.uk/view/authors/Barnett=3AJohn_Raymond=3A=3A.html>.

Bass, D. C., Cahalan, K. A., Miller-McLemore, B. J., Nierman, J. R., and Scharen, C. B., *Christian Practical Wisdom: What it is, Why it Matters* (Grand Rapids, MI: Wm. B. Eerdmans Publishing Co., 2016).

Bennett, Z., Graham, E., Pattison, S., and Walton, H., *Invitation to Research in Practical Theology* (London: Routledge, Taylor and Francis Group, 2018).

Bidwell, D. R., *When One Religion Isn't Enough: The Lives of Spiritually Fluid People* (Boston: Beacon Press, 2018).

Bolton, G., *Reflective Practice: Writing and Professional Development*, 4th edn (London: Sage Publications Ltd., 2014).

Boylorn, R. M. and Orbe, M. P. (eds), *Critical Autoethnography: Intersecting Cultural Identities in Everyday Life* (Walnut Creek: Left Coast Press Inc., 2014).

Catholic Bishops' Conference of England and Wales, *Meeting God in Friend and Stranger* (London: Catholic Truth Society, 2010), available at <https://familyofsites.bishopsconference.org.uk/plain/wp-content/uploads/sites/3/2018/11/meeting-god-friend-stranger.pdf>, accessed 26 August 2020.

Chapman, C., *Cross and Crescent: Responding to the Challenges of Islam*, 2nd edn (Nottingham: InterVarsity Press, 2007).

Cheetham, D., *Ways of Meeting and the Theology of Religions* (Farnham and Burlington: Ashgate Publishing, 2013).

Chryssides, G. D. and Gregg, S. E. (eds), *The Insider Outsider Debate: New Perspectives in the Study of Religion* (Sheffield: Equinox, 2019).

Church of England Inter-Faith Consultative Group, *Multi-Faith Worship? Questions and Suggestions from the Inter-Faith Consultative Group* (London: Church House Publishing, 1992).

Clooney, F. X., *Comparative Theology: Deep Learning across Religious Borders* (Chichester: Wiley-Blackwell, 2010).

Cole, W. O., *Teach Yourself Sikhism*, 2003 edn (London: Hodder Education, 2003).

Cole, W. O. and Sambhi, P. S., *Sikhism and Christianity: A Comparative Study* (Basingstoke: The Macmillan Press Ltd., 1993).

Cooper, J., *Cognitive Dissonance: Fifty Years of a Classic Theory* (Los Angeles, CA: Sage Publications, 2007).

Cornille, C. (ed.), *Many Mansions? Multiple Religious Belonging and Christian Identity* (Eugene, OR: Wipf and Stock Publishers, 2010).

Current Dialogue 57 (2015), December, available at <https://www.oikoumene.org/en/what-we-do/current-dialogue-magazine/currentdialogue57.pdf>, accessed 26 August 2020.

Dharam Parchar Committee, *Sikh Reht Maryada: The Code of Sikh Conduct and Conventions: English Version* (Amritsar: Dharam Parchar Committee, 2014).

Dhillon, H., *The First Sikh Spiritual Master: Timeless Wisdom from the Life and Teachings of Guru Nanak,* SkyLight Paths Quality Paperback edn (Woodstock: SkyLight Paths Publishing, 2012).

Ellis, C., *The Ethnographic I: A Methodological Novel about Autoethnography* (Walnut Creek, CA: Altmira Press, 2004).

Festinger, L., *A Theory of Cognitive Dissonance* (Stanford, CA: Stanford University Press, 1985).

Gaston, R., *A Heart Broken Open: Radical Faith in an Age of Fear* (Glasgow: Wild Goose Publications, 2009).

Gaston, R., *Faith, Hope and Love: Interfaith Engagement as Practical Theology* (London: SCM Press, 2017).

Goshen-Gottstein, A. (ed.), *Friendship Across Religions: Theological Perspectives on Interreligious Friendships* (Langham, NY: Lexington Books, 2015).

Hammersley, M. and Atkinson P., *Ethnography: Principles in Practice*, 4th edn (Abingdon: Routledge, 2019).

Hooker, P. M., *The Cross and the Khalsa: A Five Session Study Course for Christians about Sikhism* (Leamington Spa: Global Connections, 2018), available at <https://www.globalconnections.org.uk/sites/newgc.localhost/files/papers/cross_and_khalsa_0.pdf>, accessed 26 August 2020.

Hooker, R. and Lamb, C., *Love the Stranger: Christian Ministry in Multi-Faith Areas* (London: SPCK, 1986).

Jesudason, P., Rajkumar, R., and Dayam, J. P. (eds), *Many Yet One? Multiple Religious Belonging* (Geneva: World Council of Churches Publications, 2016).

Jhutti-Johal, J., *Sikhism Today* (London: Continuum International Publishing Group, 2011).

Kalsi, S. S., *Simple Guides: Sikhism*, 2007 edn (London: Bravo Ltd., 2007).

Kerney, B. L., *A Theology of Friendship*, PhD thesis, University of Durham, 2007, available at <http://etheses.dur.ac.uk/1829>, accessed 26 August 2020.

Khalsa, S. S., *The Living Guru: The Holy Sikh Scripture*, 3rd edn (Tucson, AZ: Handmade Books, n. d.).

Knitter, P. F., *Without Buddha I could not be a Christian* (London: Oneworld Publications, 2013).

Küng, H., *On Being a Christian*, tr. E. Quinn (London: Continuum, 2008).

Lawler, S., *Identity: Sociological Perspectives*, 2nd edn (Cambridge: Polity, 2014).
Lewis, C. and Cohn-Sherbok, D. (eds), *Interfaith Worship and Prayer: We Must Pray Together* (London: Jessica Kingsley Publishers, 2019).
McLaren, B. D., *Why Did Jesus, Moses, the Buddha and Mohammed Cross the Road? Christian Identity in a Multi-Faith World* (London: Hodder and Stoughton Ltd., 2012).
McLeod, W. H., *Who is a Sikh? The Problem of Sikh Identity* (Oxford: Clarendon Press, 1989).
Margalit, A., *On Betrayal* (Cambridge, MA: Harvard University Press, 2017).
Miller, S. K., *Being Both: Embracing Two Religions in One Interfaith Family* (Boston: Beacon Press, 2013).
Miller-McLemore, B. (ed.), *The Wiley-Blackwell Companion to Practical Theology* (Malden, MA, Oxford and Chichester: Wiley-Blackwell, 2012).
Moyaert, M. and Geldhof, J. (eds), *Ritual Participation and Interreligious Dialogue: Boundaries, Transgressions and Innovations* (London and New York: Bloomsbury, 2015).
Oberoi, H., *The Construction of Religious Boundaries: Culture, Identity, and Diversity in the Sikh Tradition* (Chicago, IL: The University of Chicago Press, 1994).
O'Reilly, K., *Key Concepts in Ethnography* (London: Sage, 2009).
Parry, J., *The Word of God is Not Bound* (Bangalore: Centre for Contemporary Christianity, 2009).
Pattison, S., *The Challenge of Practical Theology: Selected Essays* (London: Jessica Kingsley Publishers, 2007).
Phan, P. C., *Being Religious Interreligiously: Asian Perspectives on Interfaith Dialogue* (Maryknoll, NY: Orbis Books, 2004).
Presence and Engagement (2017), *Clergy Experiences of Evangelism and Witness in Multi-Faith Contexts: A Presence and Engagement Research Project, May–July 2016*, available at <https://www.churchofengland.org/sites/default/files/2019-05/P%26E%20Evangelism%20and%20Witness%20Report.pdf>, accessed 26 August 2020.

Race, A. and Hedges, P. (eds), *Christian Approaches to Other Faiths* (London: SCM Press, 2008).

Sarna, N., *The Book of Nanak* (Haryana: Penguin Random House India Pvt. Ltd., 2012).

Schön, D. A., *The Reflective Practitioner: How Professionals Think in Action* (New York City, NY: Basic Books, 1982).

SGPC, *Daily Hukamnama*, available at <http://dailyhukamnama.in>, accessed 26 August 2020.

Shackle, C. and Mandair, A-p. S. (eds and trans.) (2005), *Teachings of the Sikh Gurus: Selections from the Sikh Scriptures* (Abingdon: Routledge, 2005).

Singh, N.-G. K., *Sikhism: An Introduction* (London: I. B. Tauris, 2011).

Singh, P. and Fenech, L. E. (eds), *The Oxford Handbook of Sikh Studies* (Oxford: Oxford University Press, 2014).

Smith, A., *Vibrant Christianity in Multifaith Britain* (Abingdon: BRF, 2018).

Sri Guru Granth Sahib, English Version, tr. G. Singh (New Delhi: Allied Publishers PVT. Ltd., 1960).

Strange, D., *'For Their Rock is Not as Our Rock': An Evangelical Theology of Religions* (Nottingham: Apollos, 2014).

Stringer, M. D., *Contemporary Western Ethnography and the Definition of Religion* (London: Continuum, 2008).

Takhar, O. K., *Sikh Identity: An Exploration of Groups among Sikhs* (London: Routledge, 2016).

Walton, H., *Writing Methods in Theological Reflection* (London: SCM Press, 2014).

Wilson, T., *Hospitality, Service, Proclamation: Interfaith Engagement as Christian Discipleship* (London: SCM Press, 2019).

Wingate, A., *Celebrating Difference, Staying Faithful: How to Live in a Multi-Faith World* (London: Darton, Longman and Todd Ltd., 2005).

Glossary

Aarti: fire ritual where a plate with burning wicks is brought to each devotee.
Agapē: love characterized by generosity, selflessness and generality of objects.
Agapētos: beloved.
Akal Takht: "Throne of the Timeless One", the highest of five courts, set in *Harmander Sahib*, the Golden Temple, offering rulings and judgements for the worldwide Sikh community.
Akhand Paath: reading the entire *Guru Granth Sahib Ji* through without interruption.
Amicism: promotion of an initial friendliness as appropriate to interreligious and other relationships and staying open to the possibility of friendships growing in those relationships.
Amir (or *emir*): commander, general, or prince.
Amrit: a mixture of sugar and water that has been stirred with a double-edged sword. The candidates for initiation drink some of the *amrit* from the same bowl, and have it sprinkled on their eyes and hair. Each then recites the *Mool Mantra* (the fundamentals of Sikhism) and takes on the Sikh way of life, outwardly in dress and symbols, and inwardly in ethics and meditative practice.
Amritdhari: a Sikh who has received *amrit* and belongs to the *Khalsa*. He or she is expected to adopt the Five Ks, meditate regularly including before dawn, and be teetotal. Sometimes referred to in discussions with Christians as a "baptized" Sikh.
Anand karaj: Sikh marriage ceremony.
Ardas: prayer of supplication, part of daily prayer in the gurdwara.
Autoethnography: research of the interplay of introspective, personally engaged selves and cultural beliefs, practices, systems, and experiences.

Awagaun: cycle of birth and death associated with reincarnation.
Bani: religious teachings of the Sikh Gurus.
BME: Black and Minority Ethnic.
Chaur sahib: ceremonial fly whisk.
Dalits: "broken, scattered", those who have been subject to untouchability in the caste system.
Daswandh: tithing income for God's purposes.
Degh: cooking pot.
Dharma: path of righteousness.
Diocesan Interfaith Adviser (DIFA): generic term in the Church of England for all who work at diocesan level on interreligious matters.
Durbar: the court of a ruler, here used for the worship room where *Guru Granth Sahib Ji* is displayed in the gurdwara.
Ek Niwas: "one place of worship", universalist temple in the West Midlands.
Gobind Sarvar: Canada-based Sikh education programme with a gurdwara in the West Midlands.
Gora/gori: white, used of Sikh converts.
Granthi: one trained in the reading of the Sikh scriptures and employed to lead worship in the gurdwara.
Gurdwara: Sikh place for religious gathering.
Gurmukh: one who is God-oriented, and has overcome his or her ego.
Gurmukhi: language in which Sikh scriptures are written, used (with Urdu script as an alternative) to write Punjabi.
Guru Granth Sahib Ji: the Sikh scripture, the Eternal Guru.
Guru Ka Niwas: Abode of the Guru (the name of the gurdwara I attend).
Harmander Sahib: gurdwara at Amritsar, headquarters of *Sikhi* known as the "Golden Temple".
Hukam: divine order of God.
Hukamnama: word of scripture read after the *Ardas*, selected at random from *Guru Granth Sahib Ji*.
Hwyl: stirring feeling of emotional motivation and energy.
Ikk Oan Kar: symbol at the beginning of Sikh scripture, signifying "One Being Is".

Izzat: honour, family or individual prestige.
Janam-sakhi: collection of stories about the gurus.
Jap Ji: 38-stanza prayer at the beginning of *Guru Granth Sahib Ji*, attributed to Guru Nanak.
Jat: those in the traditional occupation (*zat*) of farmers.
Jathedar: cleric and judicial authority. He occupies the highest of the five *takht*s or thrones, the *Akal Takht*.
Jenoi: sacred Hindu thread worn round the wrist.
Kaccha, *Kachh* or *Kachera*: cotton underwear (one of the five signs of an *Amritdhari*).
Kanga: wooden comb (one of the five signs of an *Amritdhari*).
Kara: steel bracelet (one of the five signs of an *Amritdhari*).
Karah Parshad: warm, sweet dough made of wheat flour, sugar, and clarified butter. Distributed in the *durbar* as a sign of God's grace.
Karma: Destiny established by actions in previous lives.
Kesh: uncut hair (one of the five signs of an *Amritdhari*).
Keshdhari: person with untrimmed hair.
Khalistan: "land of the pure", objective of Sikh separatists, their own country in the Punjab region.
Khalsa: "community of the pure ones", initiated Sikhs, *Amritdhari*.
Khanda: 1. Sikh emblem in which two swords, *miri piri*, recognize the military (*amir*) and spiritual (*pir*) aspects, a central two-edged sword indicating the same balance of spirituality and practice, and the *chakra*, a circular throwing weapon suggesting eternity and wholeness (having replaced the *degh*). 2. two-edged sword found at the centre of the Sikh emblem.
Kirat karna: providing for one's family by working for a living.
Kirpan: steel sword (one of the five signs of an *Amritdhari*).
Kirtan: Sikh devotional singing, usually in the gurdwara.
Langar: communal meal which all share at the gurdwara.
Lohar: social grouping associated with blacksmiths.
Manmukh: self-oriented, an ignorant person bound by desires, ego, and worldly concerns.
Maranatha: Aramaic for "Come, Lord" or "Our Lord has come" (1 Corinthians 16:22), used as a mantra by the World Community for Christian Meditation.

Miri piri: two outer swords in the *khanda*, signifying the military (*amir*) and spiritual (*pir*) aspects of *Sikhi*.
Misl: originally sovereign states of the Sikh confederacy, now descendants of a military unit.
Mona: Sikh who cuts his or her hair (abusive term).
Mool Mantra or *Mul Mantra*: first verse of *Guru Granth Sahib Ji*, encapsulating Sikh teaching.
MRB: Multiple Religious Belonging.
MRP: Multiple Religious Participation.
Mukti: liberation of the soul from transmigration.
Naam Karan: Sikh ceremony for naming a child.
Nirgun sargun: conundrum that God is both with and without attributes.
Nirvair: without enmity, a divine attribute.
Nishan sahib: symbol, referring to a triangular flag, properly yellow but usually orange, incorporating the *khanda*, usually on a high flagpole outside a gurdwara.
Orientalism: attitude to Eastern societies embedded in Western culture, part of a strategy to give Westerners the upper hand.
Pangat: a synonym for *langar*, the communal meal which all share at the gurdwara, used to draw attention to the equality and mingling of all participants.
Panj pyare: five beloved, first five initiates of the *Khalsa*, thence five initiates who administer *amrit* to others, and five initiates representing the originals in parades etc.
Parchar: Sikh evangelistic street mission.
Patit: lapsed *Khalsa* Sikh.
Philia: affectionate love, as of a brother or friend.
Pir: "elder", Muslim holy man.
Prasad: food-offering to God, consumed after worship.
Presence and Engagement: Church of England's programme for equipping Christians for multi-faith mission and ministry.
Programme: special worship and social event at a gurdwara.
Puja: Hindu prayer ritual.
Punjabiat: cultural heritage and ethos of the people of the Punjab and their descendants.

Ramgarhia: *misl* named after Jassa Singh Ramgarhia, a carpenter put in charge of building a fort near Amritsar, who then became leader of the *misl* charged with protecting *Harmander Sahib*.

Ravidassi: followers of Guru Ravidass, a contributor to *Guru Granth Sahib Ji* and an untouchable. Relations with mainstream Sikhs are problematic.

Rehat Maryada: *Khalsa* guide for the Sikh way of life covering religious rites and ethical observances.

Sach khand: bedroom where *Guru Granth Sahib Ji* is put to rest at night.

Sahajdhari: non-*Khalsa* Sikhs, sometimes referred to insensitively as "slow adopters".

Salaat: Muslim devotional liturgy oriented toward Mecca.

Salwar Kameez: trouser suit worn in Pakistan and India by women and men.

Sangat: Sikh congregation.

Sant: (generally) a human being revered for his or her knowledge of "self, truth, reality" and as a "truth-exemplar". (In Sikhism) a being who has attained spiritual enlightenment and divine knowledge and power through union with God.

Sant Nirankari: worshippers of the Formless One with their own living guru and a problematic relationship with *Sikhi*.

Shahada: Muslim testament of faith.

Shiromani Gurdwara Parbandhak Committee: manages gurdwaras in Punjab, Haryana, Himachal Pradesh, and Chandigarh, and administers *Harmandir Sahib*.

Shukriya: thank you.

Sikhi: Sikhism, but underscoring the multiple ways of being Sikh.

Simran: meditation on *Waheguru*.

Singh Sabha: nineteenth-century Sikh revivalist movement.

Siropa: honorific scarf.

Sukhmani Sahib: "jewel of peace", hymn of blessing by Guru Arjan.

Superdiversity: A state reflecting movements of people from many different ethnicities, languages, and nations and a growing complexity about where, how, and with whom people live.

Tabla: pair of small drums.

Takhat: throne or seat of power, in which *Guru Granth Sahib Ji* is presented.
Takht: judgement seat in one of the five leading gurdwaras.
Tankah: breach of Khala discipline calling for community service, not re-initiation.
Tarkhan: social grouping associated with carpentry.
Theodicy: Theology that attempts to vindicate an omnipotent and omniscient God in the face of the evident problem of evil.
Übersehen: to see through.
Vaisakhi: celebration of anniversary of founding of the *Khalsa*, April 13th or 14th.
Waand chhakna (or *vand ke chakna*): sharing of one's earnings.
Waheguru: Wonderful One, a term used by Sikhs for the absolute.
Waheguru ji ka Kalsa, Waheguru ji ki fateh: "the *Khalsa* belongs to God, victory is the gift of God", Sikh greeting and response.
Yagnopavitam: Hindu thread ceremony marking initiation.
Yeshu Satsang: groups of Christian converts consciously retaining Sikh or Hindu social structures.
Zat: group with a traditional occupation.

Notes

1. I have followed the practice of using "*Sikhi*" (also spelled *Sikkhi*) instead of "Sikhism" to indicate awareness of the multiple ways of being Sikh and the complexity of Sikh identity beyond religious belief.
2. Although my mother's grandmother came from a well-to-do family of bakers in Worcester, sharing their reserved pew in the cathedral until she eloped with the postman to Birmingham.
3. J. A. T. Robinson, *Honest to God* (London: SCM Press, 1963).
4. From my own note at the time. Any quotation without an attached reference is from my own notes of various occasions and meetings made near the time.
5. Smethwick Galton Bridge station, if you are reading this.
6. Which as well as Wolverhampton itself includes Walsall, West Bromwich and some other parts of the Black Country, as well as areas of South Staffordshire including Lichfield and Tamworth. I was later also appointed interfaith adviser to the Bishop of Lichfield.
7. "Interfaith" is the term used by the Church of England. I use it here in the narrower context of professional discussion, but generally prefer the term "interreligious", as acknowledging the broader communal and cultural aspects of the engagement.
8. L. Casey, *A Review into Opportunity and Integration* (London: Department of Communities and Local Government, 2016), p. 149, her quotation marks.
9. S. Vukalić, "The Courage to Remember", in *Remembering Srebrenica*, available at <https://www.srebrenica.org.uk/survivor-stories/the-courage-to-remember-safet-vukalic/>, accessed 3 March 2018.
10. M. Volf, *Exclusion and Embrace: A Theological Exploration of Identity, Otherness, and Reconciliation* (Nashville: Abingdon Press, 1996), p. 282.
11. J. R. Barnett, "Christian Dream Interpretation: Awakening the Interest of Practical Theologians", in N. Rooms and Z. Bennett (eds), *Practical Theology in Progress: Showcasing an Emerging Discipline* (Abingdon: Routledge, 2018).
12. Shri Venkateswara (Balaji) Temple, Tividale.

13 R. Eddo-Lodge, *Why I am No Longer Talking to White People about Race*, extended edition (London: Bloomsbury, 2018), pp. 19–20.
14 J. V. Bragt, "Multiple Religious Belonging of the Japanese People", in C. Cornille (ed.), *Many Mansions? Multiple Religious Belonging and Christian Identity* (Eugene, OR: Wipf and Stock, 2010), pp. 7–19, p. 10.
15 S. K. Miller, *Being Both: Embracing Two Religions in One Interfaith Family* (Boston: Beacon Press, 2013).
16 J. Geldhof, "Epilogue: Inter-riting as a Peculiar Form of Love", in M. Moyaert and J. Geldhof (eds), *Ritual Participation and Interreligious Dialogue: Boundaries, Transgressions and Innovations* (London and New York: Bloomsbury, 2015), pp. 218–23, here at pp. 222–3.
17 A state reflecting movements of people from many different ethnicities, languages and nations and a growing complexity about where, how and with whom people live.
18 T. Ryan, *Interreligious Prayer: A Christian Guide* (New York and Mahwah, NJ: Paulist Press, 2008), p. 1.
19 Catholic Bishops' Conference of England and Wales, *Meeting God in Friend and Stranger* (London: Catholic Truth Society, 2010), p. 51, available at <https://familyofsites.bishopsconference.org.uk/plain/wp-content/uploads/sites/3/2018/11/meeting-god-friend-stranger.pdf>, accessed 7 July 2020.
20 P. J. R. Rajkumar (ed.), *Current Dialogue 57* (Geneva: World Council of Churches, 2015), available at <https://www.oikoumene.org/en/what-we-do/current-dialogue-magazine/currentdialogue57.pdf>, accessed 27 October 2017; P. Jesudason, R. Rajkumar and J. P. Dayam (eds), *Many Yet One? Multiple Religious Belonging* (Geneva: World Council of Churches Publications, 2016).
21 P. Jesudason, R. Rajkumar and J. P. Dayam, "Introduction", in P. Jesudason, R. Rajkumar and J. P. Dayam (eds), *Many Yet One?*, pp. 1–4 at p. 4.
22 Church of England Inter-Faith Consultative Group, *Multi-Faith Worship? Questions and Suggestions from the Inter-Faith Consultative Group* (London: Church House Publishing, 1992).
23 Presence and Engagement (2017), *Clergy Experiences of Evangelism and Witness in Multi-Faith Contexts. A Presence and Engagement Research Project, May–July 2016*, pp. 3f., available at <https://www.churchofengland.org/sites/default/files/2019-05/P%26E%20Evangelism%20and%20Witness%20Report.pdf>, accessed 7 July 2020.
24 See in Chapter 8 the difficulties felt over this issue by interfaith advisers.

25   C. Lewis, "The Argument for Interfaith Prayer and Worship", in C. Lewis and D. Cohn-Sherbok (eds), *Interfaith Worship and Prayer: We Must Pray Together* (London: Jessica Kingsley Publishers, 2019), pp. 17–31.
26   R. Hooker and C. Lamb, *Love the Stranger: Christian Ministry in Multi-Faith Areas* (London: SPCK, 1986); A. Wingate, *Celebrating Difference, Staying Faithful: How to Live in a Multi-Faith World* (London: Darton, Longman and Todd Ltd., 2005); C. Chapman, *Cross and Crescent: Responding to the Challenges of Islam*, second edition (Nottingham: InterVarsity Press, 2007); R. Sudworth, *Distinctly Welcoming: Christian Presence in a Multifaith Society* (Bletchley: Scripture Union, 2007); R. Gaston, *A Heart Broken Open: Radical Faith in an Age of Fear* (Glasgow: Wild Goose Publications, 2009); T. Wilson, *Hospitality, Service, Proclamation: Interfaith Engagement as Christian Discipleship* (London: SCM Press, 2019); A. Smith, *Vibrant Christianity in Multifaith Britain* (Abington: BRF, 2018).
27   D. Premawardhana, "The Unremarkable Hybrid: Aloysius Pieris and the Redundancy of Multiple Religious Belonging", *Journal of Ecumenical Studies* 46:1 (2011), pp. 76–89; P. F. Knitter, *No Other Name? A Critical Survey of Christian Attitudes Toward the World Religions* (Maryknoll, NY: Orbis Books, 1985); C. Geffré, "Double Belonging and the Originality of Christianity as a Religion", in C. Cornille (ed.), *Many Mansions?*, pp. 93–105; M. Voss Roberts, "Religious Belonging and the Multiple Author(s)", *Journal of Feminist Studies in Religion* 26:1 (2010), pp. 43–62.
28   Later reversed following a change of membership criteria.
29   E. Said, *Orientalism* (London: Penguin Books, 2003), p. xxii.
30   BBC (2017), "Resurrection did not happen, say quarter of Christians", available at: <https://www.bbc.co.uk/news/uk-england-39153121>, accessed 27 April 2017.
31   A stirring feeling of emotional motivation and energy (Welsh).
32   "Christ be with me, Christ within me, Christ behind me, Christ before me, Christ beside me, Christ to win me, Christ to comfort and restore me; Christ beneath me, Christ above me, Christ in quiet, Christ in danger, Christ in hearts of all that love me, Christ in mouth of friend and stranger."
33   "Abode of the Guru".
34   I use the past tense to describe my engagement with Beacon Church, which ceased on retirement, but use the present tense to describe observations in

the gurdwara as I am still attending, although that is currently interrupted by COVID-19 restrictions.

35 At church I also make a donation, by standing order.

36 In the 1662 Book of Common Prayer wedding service, the groom worships the bride—he gives her true value—as he gives her the ring: "[. . . w]ith this ring I thee wed, with my body I thee worship . . . ".

37 On reading this, Devsi commented: "Every country is changing on this. For example, formerly you would touch a child on entering a family situation, but not now in Britain. Men and women can sit together in the older gurdwaras in India, but now women prefer not to be touched by men."

38 Trouser suit commonly worn in Pakistan and India.

39 Pair of small drums.

40 Said in such a way as to only take two syllables: "Wah Gru".

41 *Kirpan*: knife. The word is derived from *kirpa*, "kindness", and *an*, "honour". The *kirpan* should be used with kindness and honour, for justice not aggression—Devsi.

42 Or two letters. One of my Punjabi Sikh interviewees regarded this as an old-fashioned way of choosing a name. He had chosen his child's names independently.

43 *Seva*: service which is performed without any expectation of reward.

44 I was told more than once about a poet attending a gurdwara who was chided for joining in the washing up. He replied: "I am not washing the dishes but my soul."

45 *Amrit:* a mixture of sugar and water that has been stirred with a double-edged sword, the drinking of which is the main action in Sikh initiation.

46 *Sri Guru Granth Sahib English Version* in four volumes, tr. G. Singh (New Delhi: Allied Publishers PVT Ltd., 1960), p. 599. (References are given in page numbers as standardized for *Guru Granth Sahib Ji.*)

47 They may be more earnest about it than some; they told me their service lasted three hours because of all the teaching, as contrasted with a more normal service of between thirty and forty-five minutes.

48 West Midlands Police circulated a warning around gurdwaras that the gold on display was tempting robbers.

49 Food-offering to God, consumed after worship.

50. Methodist Conference, *The Constitutional Practice and Discipline of the Methodist Church* SO 700ff, available at <https://www.methodist.org.uk/for-churches/governance/cpd/>, pp. 548ff., accessed 7 July 2019.
51. Punjabi/Gurmukhi is a stronger oral than written culture. See *British Sikh Report* (2014), pp. 21f. available at <https://britishsikhreport.org/british-sikh-report-download-2014/>, accessed 7 July 2020. Sathnam Sanghera, a second-generation Punjabi from Wolverhampton, has written: "Punjabi, the language my parents speak [though his father could not read or write in it], is the one I learnt first. However, I left home nearly twelve years ago and have since become less and less proficient in it, so much so that now, even asking for a glass of water sometimes has me burbling incoherently." S. Sanghera, *The Boy with a Top-knot: A Memoir of Love, Secrets and Lies in Wolverhampton* (London: Penguin Books, 2009), p. 21.
52. *Amritdhari*: a Sikh who has received *amrit* and belongs to the *Khalsa*. He or she is expected to adopt the Five Ks, meditate regularly including before dawn, and be teetotal. Sometimes referred to in discussions with Christians as a "baptized" Sikh.
53. They eventually started at the end of 2019.
54. N. Mehat with M. Wardell, *When Love Prevails: A Sikh Woman Finds Christ* (Carlisle: O. M. Publishing (Carlisle: Paternoster Press), 1998).
55. H. Montefiore, *Reclaiming the High Ground: A Christian Response to Secularism* (Basingstoke: The Macmillan Press Ltd., 1990), pp. 126–8.
56. Pew Forum (2009), "Many Americans Mix Multiple Faiths", available at <https://www.pewforum.org/2009/12/09/many-americans-mix-multiple-faiths/>, accessed 11 March 2016; ComRes Global (2017), *BBC Religion and Ethics Polling*, available at: <https://faithsurvey.co.uk/download/uk-religion-survey.pdf>, accessed 23 November 2017, p. 7.
57. M. D. Stringer, *Contemporary Western Ethnography and the Definition of Religion* (London: Continuum, 2008), pp. 38–9.
58. J. Parry, *The Word of God is Not Bound* (Bangalore: Centre for Contemporary Christianity, 2009), p. 220.
59. Dharam Parchar Committee, *Sikh Reht Maryada: The Code of Sikh Conduct and Conventions. English Version* (Amritsar: Dharam Parchar Committee, 2014), p. 7.
60. K. Rand, "Navigating Multiplicity in a Binary World: Complex Religious Identity in Java", in G. D. Chryssides and S. E. Gregg (eds), *The Insider*

61. *Outsider Debate: New Perspectives in the Study of Religion* (Sheffield: Equinox, 2019), pp. 270–90; J. Cooper, *Cognitive Dissonance: Fifty Years of a Classic Theory* (Los Angeles, CA: Sage Publications, 2007), p. 82.
61. Stringer, *Contemporary Western Ethnography and the Definition of Religion*, p. 38.
62. See Chapter 3.
63. Not her real name.
64. *Waheguru*: "The Wonderful One", a term used by Sikhs for the Absolute and used in *simran*, meditation. *Maranatha*: Aramaic word meaning "come Lord" or "our Lord has come" (1 Corinthians 16:22), used as a mantra by the World Community for Christian Meditation. I used them in this way to bring Sikh and Christian meditation together.
65. Church of England Inter-Faith Consultative Group, *Multi-Faith Worship? Questions and Suggestions from the Inter-Faith Consultative Group*, p. 32.
66. A. Margalit, *On Betrayal* (Cambridge, MA: Harvard University Press, 2017).
67. Quoted in F. Austin, *The Language of the Metaphysical Poets (Language of Literature)* (London: Palgrave, 1992), p. 127 [Traherne's punctuation].
68. S. K. Miller, *Being Both: Embracing Two Religions in One Interfaith Family* (Boston, MA: Beacon Press, 2013).
69. There is an alternative reading that no-one is truly following their own religion.
70. G. W. Hughes, *God of Surprises*, 2nd edn. (London: Darton, Longman and Todd, 2008), p. xvi.
71. A cynical Sikh interviewee later seemed to confirm this, saying generally about *gora* attending gurdwaras: "That is why they won't go any further with you. You know more than them and they will back off, they have no more to say to you." But this runs counter to my experience of many Sikhs being able to talk about their beliefs from a background of considerable knowledge and sophistication.
72. But see Ray Gaston's interpretation of the Babel myth as one of liberation from the oppressive imposition of uniformity, celebrating diversity: R. Gaston, *Faith, Hope and Love: Interfaith Engagement as Practical Theology* (London: SCM Press, 2017), pp. 127–31.
73. Devsi commented on reading this: "The question 'what are we going to get out of it?' usually refers to money. You have answered that now, you will publicize the name of GKN, what more can you have?"

74 My interfaith duties precluded my avoiding halal meat, as do 44 per cent of British Sikh meat-eaters.
75 D. Strange, 'For Their Rock is Not as Our Rock': An Evangelical Theology of Religions (Nottingham: Apollos, 2014), p. 41.
76 Being raised in the multi-religious setting of Guyana has led Dan Strange and Michael Jagessar in opposite directions over interreligious relations, but neither reflects on why. It is presented as not relevant by Strange, obviously formative by Jagessar.
77 Not his real name.
78 Elisha sent a messenger to [Naaman], saying, "Go, wash in the Jordan seven times, and your flesh shall be restored and you shall be clean." But Naaman became angry and went away, saying, "I thought that for me he would surely come out, and stand and call on the name of the Lord his God, and would wave his hand over the spot, and cure the leprosy! Are not Abana and Pharpar, the rivers of Damascus, better than all the waters of Israel? Could I not wash in them, and be clean? He turned and went away in a rage" (2 Kings 5:10–12).
79 Stringer, Contemporary Western Ethnography and the Definition of Religion.
80 S. Pattison, "Spirituality and Spiritual Care Made Simple: A Suggestive, Normative and Essentialist Approach", Practical Theology 3:3 (2010), pp. 351–66, here at p. 353.
81 British Sikh Report (2017), available at <http://britishsikhreport.org/wp-content/uploads/2017/03/British-Sikh-Report-2017-Online.pdf>, accessed 4 December 2017, p. 20.
82 O. K. Takhar, "Sikhi(sm) and the Twenty-First Century Diaspora", in C. Lewis and D. Cohn-Sherbok (eds), Sensible Religion (Abingdon: Routledge, 2016), pp. 167–80, here at p. 169.
83 W. H. McLeod, Who is a Sikh? The Problem of Sikh Identity (Oxford: Clarendon Press, 1989), pp. 90–3.
84 H. Oberoi, The Construction of Religious Boundaries: Culture, Identity, and Diversity in the Sikh Tradition (Chicago, IL: University of Chicago Press, 1994).
85 P. Singh, "An Overview of Sikh History", in P. Singh and L. E. Fenech (eds), The Oxford Handbook of Sikh Studies (Oxford: Oxford University Press, 2014), pp. 19–34; H. Singh, "'Western' Writers on the Sikhs", in P. Singh and L. E. Fenech (eds), The Oxford Handbook of Sikh Studies, pp. 201–11.

86. J. Parry, "Sikhism: From Competition to Co-operation", in A. Race and P. M. Hedges (eds), *Christian Approaches to Other Faiths* (London: SCM Press, 2008), pp. 255–68, here at p. 255.
87. Although there is a tradition of Guru Nanak going to the Vatican in 1520 and arguing against slavery.
88. Although it is echoed by *Yeshu Satsang*, groups of Christian converts consciously retaining Sikh or Hindu social structures.
89. J. Parry, *The Word of God is Not Bound*.
90. Described at the time by Wesley Ariarajah, then Director of Interreligious Relations at the World Council of Churches, as the only conversation in the world between Sikhs and any Christian denomination.
91. W. O. Cole and P. S. Sambhi, *Sikhism and Christianity: A Comparative Study* (Basingstoke: Macmillan, 1993).
92. R. Lambert, *What Might Christians Learn, Theologically and Pastorally, from Christian-Sikh Encounter?* Unpublished M. A. dissertation, University of Nottingham, 2001; Scriptural Reasoning (2017), *Scriptural Reasoning Now*. Available at <http://www.scripturalreasoning.org/scriptural-reasoning-now.html>, accessed 27 December 2017.
93. Material that clearly had Christian sectarian origins, now borrowed by Sikh polemicists.
94. P. Singh, "'The Whole World Sings to Your Glory Day and Night': Sikh Response towards Interfaith Worship and Prayer", in C. Lewis and D. Cohn-Sherbok (eds), *Interfaith Worship and Prayer: We Must Pray Together*, pp. 208–16.
95. K. P. Sian, *Unsettling Sikh and Muslim Conflict: Mistaken Identities, Forced Conversions, and Postcolonial Formations* (Plymouth: Lexington Publications, 2013).
96. K. Purohit, "Anger Among Sikhs in Britain Raises the Heat on UK-India Ties", *Asia Times* 6 March 2018, available at <https://asiatimes.com/2018/03/anger-among-sikhs-britain-raises-heat-uk-india-ties/>, accessed 7 July 2020.
97. *Dharma*: Path of Righteousness.
98. H. Sherwood, "Justin Welby Says he is 'Sorry and Ashamed' over Church's Racism", *Guardian*, 11 February 2020, available at <https://www.theguardian.com/world/2020/feb/11/justin-welby-tells-synod-he-is-sorry-and-ashamed-over-churchs-racism>, accessed 14 March 2020.

99. *Ravidassi*: followers of Guru Ravidass, a contributor to *Guru Granth Sahib Ji* and an untouchable. Relations with mainstream Sikhs are problematic.
100. O. K. Takhar, *Sikh Identity: An Exploration of Groups among Sikhs* (London: Routledge, 2016), p. 3.
101. K. Sato, "Divisions among Sikh Communities in Britain and the Role of the Caste System: A Case Study of Four Gurdwaras in Multi-ethnic Leicester", *Journal of Punjab Studies* 19:1 (2011), pp. 1–26, available at <https://punjab.global.ucsb.edu/sites/secure.lsit.ucsb.edu.gisp.d7_sp/files/sitefiles/journals/volume19/no1/1-KiytakaSatoCasteDivisionsinLeicester.pdf>, accessed 28 December 2017.
102. J. Jhutti-Johal, *Sikhism Today* (London: Continuum, 2013), pp. 79–81. Thirty-six per cent of British Asians find same-sex relationships unacceptable, as against 15 per cent of the wider population: BBC (2018), "British Asians more socially conservative than rest of UK, survey suggests", available at <https://www.bbc.co.uk/news/uk-45133717>, accessed 18 August 2018.
103. J. Alison, *On Being Liked* (London: Darton, Longman and Todd Ltd., 2003), p. xi; M. Voss Roberts, "Queering Multiple Religious Belonging", *Journal of Feminist Studies in Religion* (2016), available at <http://www.fsrinc.org/queering-multiple-religious-belonging/>, accessed 2 December 2017.
104. C. A. Davies, *Reflexive Ethnography: A Guide to Researching Selves and Others*, second edition (London: Routledge, Taylor and Francis, 2008), p. 49.
105. Jhutti-Johal, *Sikhism Today*, pp. 38–9.
106. In 2017, 45 per cent of British Sikh women were graduates and 23 per cent had a postgraduate qualification, slightly more than among their male counterparts at 44 per cent and 22 per cent respectively. See *British Sikh Report* (2017), p. 26, available at <http://britishsikhreport.org/wp-content/uploads/2017/03/British-Sikh-Report-2017-Online.pdf>, accessed 4 December 2017.
107. J. Sanghera, *Shame: The True Story of a Girl's Struggle to Survive* (London: Hodder and Stoughton, 2007); S. Sanghera, *The Boy with a Top-knot*; N. Puri, "The hidden plight of Asian women", available at <http://news.bbc.co.uk/1/hi/6290868.stm>, accessed 27 December 2017; Sikh Helpline (2017), *What Do We Do?* Available at <https://www.sikhhelpline.com/>, accessed 27 December 2017.
108. Jhutti-Johal, *Sikhism Today*, p. 47.

[109] L. Mulvey, "Visual Pleasure and Narrative Cinema", *Screen* 16:3 (1975), pp. 6–18.

[110] A. Coffey, *The Ethnographic Self: Fieldwork and the Representation of Identity* (London: Sage, 1999), p. 13.

[111] Three women for every two men in the UK (See Pew Forum (2016), "The Gender Gap in Religion Around the World", available at <https://www.pewforum.org/2016/03/22/the-gender-gap-in-religion-around-the-world/>, accessed 7 July 2020); there are twice as many women as men at Beacon Church.

[112] H. Küng, *On Being a Christian*, tr. E. Quinn (London: Continuum, 2008), p. 569.

[113] H. U. von Balthasar, *Who is a Christian?*, tr. F. Davidson, fifth edition (San Francisco, CA: Ignatius Press, 2014), pp. 102, 107, 114–7.

[114] R. Panikkar, "On Christian Identity: Who is a Christian?", in C. Cornille (ed.), *Many Mansions?*, pp. 121–41.

[115] Each entry is ordered first by the tune set for that piece, then by author, gurus first then other *sants* (who may or may not be Sikh), then by its metric form, with the longer pieces first. There is an introduction of three liturgical prayers and an epilogue of miscellaneous works.

[116] Though the experience is not the aim. The same interviewee had said, "People do different kinds of meditation, mostly for feeling good. *Simran* is different in that you do it in order to meet God."

[117] The emblem also includes a two-edged sword, also known as the *khanda*, indicating the same balance of spirituality and practice, and the *chakka*, a circular throwing weapon suggesting eternity and wholeness. The *chakka* has come to replace the earlier *degh*, or cooking pot (M. Hawley, "Sikh Institutions", in P. Singh and L. E. Fenech (eds), *The Oxford Handbook of Sikh Studies*, pp. 317–26, here at p. 324).

[118] Using the present tense as I continue to be engaged with this group, although this has been disrupted by COVID-19.

[119] From the festival of Lessons and Carols.

[120] Going just beyond a round number is a Punjabi tradition explained as signifying a "more than" approach to giving.

[121] On reading this, Devsi recalled (which I did not) my asking, "If I want to take *amrit* who do I have to get permission from?" He apparently replied: "You don't need permission from anyone; it's like an open university. I will not

force people to become Sikh, but I will welcome them. I can't just say 'he's a white man!' He's a Sikh, and he has done the study. You don't just become by attending, you learn, even if born a Sikh."

[122] *Hukam*: divine order of God.
[123] I. Bhogal, Interview with the Author, 5 April 2017.
[124] S. Pattison, *The Challenge of Practical Theology: Selected Essays* (London: Jessica Kingsley Publishers, 2007), pp. 229–42.
[125] It is an awkward choice phonetically. "Sikh-Christian" with the "K-Ch" sound does not flow as easily as "Christian-Sikh", and "Christian" sounds more adjectival than "Sikh", though both can be adjective or noun.
[126] D. A. Schön, *The Reflective Practitioner: How Professionals Think in Action* (New York City, NY: Basic Books, 1982), p. 50.
[127] I have also included three comments relevant to this section from one of my interviewees, a Christian priest who attends a yoga class. These comments are identified.
[128] Hindu fire ritual where a plate with burning wicks is brought to each devotee.
[129] Hindu prayer ritual.
[130] Muslim devotional liturgy oriented toward Mecca.
[131] It is not only the humble DIFA who has been drawn spontaneously into the worship practices of another religion. In May 1999, to the surprise of all present and the consternation of his entourage, Pope John Paul II reverently kissed a Qur'an that was presented to him. Despite repeated attacks over it he never offered any explanation, leaving the impression that it was a matter of religious instinct rather than policy.
[132] Letters in brackets refer to the paragraphs above.
[133] Except for one contributor, a Christian Buddhist, for whom the focus of discernment was ethical.
[134] Catholic Bishops' Conference of England and Wales, *Meeting God in Friend and Stranger*, p. 51.
[135] H. Sherwood, "Zen Group to Stop York Minster Meetings after Religious Row", *The Guardian,* 16 July 2019, accessed at <https://www.theguardian.com/world/2019/jul/16/zen-group-york-minster-meetings-religious-row> on 10 August 2020. See also C. Collingwood, *Zen Wisdom for Christians* (London: Jessica Kingsley Publishers, 2019).
[136] J. I. Tu, "Episcopal Priest Ann Holmes Redding has been Defrocked", *The Seattle Times,* 1 April 2009. Available at <https://www.seattletimes.com/

seattle-news/episcopal-priest-ann-holmes-redding-has-been-defrocked/>, accessed 10 July 2018.

137. Tu, "Episcopal Priest Ann Holmes Redding has been Defrocked".

138. Gamaliel advised the Jewish court not to persecute Christians: "So in the present case, I tell you, keep away from these men and let them alone; because if this plan or this undertaking is of human origin, it will fail; but if it is of God, you will not be able to overthrow them—in that case you may even be found fighting against God!" (Acts 5:38).

139. There are plenty of places where they are lined up in an identity parade of holy people, e.g. Sai Baba Mandir, Lonsdale Rd., Wolverhampton. The poster *Let's Peace Together Our World* by Vik Kainth has a line-up of faith leaders including Jesus and Nanak where mutual love is implied by a heart shape at each joining of hands, but the subjects are not otherwise relating.

140. K. O'Brien, *The Ignatian Adventure* (Chicago, IL: Loyola Press, 2011), pp. 14–15; F. X. Clooney, *Comparative Theology: Deep Learning across Religious Borders* (Chichester: Wiley-Blackwell, 2010), p. 54.

141. R. W. Funk and the Jesus Seminar, *The Gospel of Jesus According to the Jesus Seminar* (Santa Rosa, CA: Polebridge Press, 1999); S. Sarna, *The Book of Nanak* (Haryana: Penguin Random House India Pvt. Ltd., 2012).

142. Path of righteousness.

143. The buffaloes had trampled the neighbour's crops, but when the furious neighbour took Nanak's father to see the damage all was restored as though nothing had happened.

144. Nanak's musician and companion.

145. *Sant*: (generally) a human being revered for his or her knowledge of "self, truth, reality" and as a "truth-exemplar". (In Sikhism) a being who has attained spiritual enlightenment and divine knowledge and power through union with God.

146. G. C. Meilaender, *Friendship: A Study in Theological Ethics* (Notre Dame, IN: University of Notre Dame Press, 1985), p. 105.

147. B. L. Kerney, *A Theology of Friendship*, PhD thesis, University of Durham, 2007, available at <http://etheses.dur.ac.uk/1829/1/1829.pdf>, downloaded 23 February 2017, p. 38.

148. Aelred of Rievaulx, *Spiritual Friendship*, tr. L. C. Braceland (Collegeville, MN: Liturgical Press, 2010), p. 66.

[149] M. L. Dutton, "Introduction", in Aelred of Rievaulx, *Spiritual Friendship*, pp. 13–50, 34–7.

[150] Aelred of Rievaulx, *Spiritual Friendship*, pp. 102–6.

[151] H. Dhillon, *The First Sikh Spiritual Master: Timeless Wisdom from the Life and Teachings of Guru Nanak*, SkyLight Paths Quality Paperback Edition (Woodstock: SkyLight Paths Publishing, 2012), p. vi.

[152] Dhillon, *The First Sikh Spiritual Master*, pp. 22, 70.

[153] B. S. Dhillon, "Sikh Perspective on Friendship: Inside View", in A. Goshen-Gottstein (ed.), *Friendship Across Religions: Theological Perspectives on Interreligious Friendships* (Langham, NY: Lexington Books, 2015), pp. 135–44, 137–8, 142; E. Nesbitt, "Interreligious Friendship: Insights from the Sikh Tradition", in A. Goshen-Gottstein (ed.), *Friendship Across Religions*, pp. 117–34, 121–2.

[154] S. S. Juss, "The Secular Tradition in Sikhism", *Rutgers Journal of Law and Religion* 11:2 (2010), pp. 270–357, 280.

[155] Aelred of Rievaulx, *Spiritual Friendship*, p. 126.

[156] Alison, *On Being Liked*, pp. 1, 14–16, 143; S. McFague, *Models of God: Theology for an Ecological, Nuclear Age* (Philadelphia, PA: Fortress Press, 1987), pp. 165, 167.

[157] *Sri Guru Granth Sahib English Version* in four volumes, tr. G. Singh, p. 958.

[158] *Sri Guru Granth Sahib English Version* in four volumes, tr. G. Singh, p. 1421.

[159] Theology that attempts to vindicate an omnipotent and omniscient God in the face of the evident problem of evil.

[160] M. P. Galupo and K. A. Gonzalez, "Friendship Values and Cross-Category Friendships: Understanding Adult Friendship Patterns Across Gender, Sexual Orientation and Race", *Sex Roles* 68:11–12 (2013), pp. 779–90. N.B. "Ritual" is being used by the authors in a non-religious sense. P.-W. Lee, "Bridging Cultures: Understanding the Construction of Relational Identity in Intercultural Friendship", *Journal of Intercultural Communication Research* 35:1 (2006), pp. 3–22.

[161] Nesbitt, "Interreligious Friendship: Insights from the Sikh Tradition", in A. Goshen-Gottstein (ed.), *Friendship Across Religions*.

[162] Mark 1:1–11; C. M. Tuckett, "Mark", in J. Muddiman and J. Barton (eds), *The Oxford Bible Commentary: The Gospels* (Oxford: Oxford University Press, 2001), pp. 84–134, 87.

[163] R. Gidoomal and M. Wardell, *Lions, Princesses, Gurus: Reaching Your Sikh Neighbour* (Godalming: Highland Books, 1996), pp. 152, 156; A. Goshen-Gottstein (ed.), *Friendship Across Religions*, p. xxxvii.

[164] W. Apel, *Signs of Peace: The Interfaith Letters of Thomas Merton* (Maryknoll, NY: Orbis Books, 2006), pp. xix, 137; J. M. Vento, "The Sacramentality of Interreligious Friendship", in A. Goshen-Gottstein (ed.), *Friendship Across Religions*, pp. 69–75.

[165] B. D. McLaren, *Why Did Jesus, Moses, the Buddha and Mohammed Cross the Road? Christian Identity in a Multi-Faith World* (London: Hodder and Stoughton Ltd, 2012), pp. 2–5, 60–7.

[166] G. Kittel and F. Friedrich (eds), *Theological Dictionary of the New Testament Abridged in One Volume*, tr. and abr. G. W. Bromley (Grand Rapids, MI: William B. Eerdmans Publishing Company, 1985), p. 5.

[167] For example, OED accessed 1 February 2018.

[168] V. A. Thompson, *The Problem of Administrative Compassion: Without Sympathy or Enthusiasm* (Tuscaloosa, AL: University of Alabama Press, 2007), p. 20.

[169] A. K. Anthony and J. McCabe, "Friendship Talk as Identity Work: Defining the Self through Friend Relations", *Symbolic Interaction* 38:1 (2015), pp. 64–82.

[170] D. Cheetham, *Ways of Meeting and the Theology of Religions* (Farnham and Burlington: Ashgate Publishing, 2013), pp. 90, 118, 119, 146–8.

[171] Cheetham, *Ways of Meeting*, pp. 6–7.

[172] Cheetham, *Ways of Meeting*, pp. 11, 16.

[173] Steadfast love and faithfulness will meet;/righteousness and peace will kiss each other. Faithfulness will spring up from the ground,/and righteousness will look down from the sky.

[174] G. D. Chryssides and S. E. Gregg (eds), *The Insider Outsider Debate*.

[175] See *Sri Guru Granth Sahib English Version 1960*, p. 974. (Standard page no.)

[176] *British Sikh Report* (2013), available at <http://britishsikhreport.org/wp-content/uploads/2013/06/BSR_2013_FINAL.pdf>, accessed 19 June 2015, p. 23.

[177] The discrepancy arose when I was away from home and could get to a church but not to a gurdwara.

[178] The original collocutor had to withdraw, leading to a break until another took it on.

179 Over *amritdhari* not all being vegetarian, over my asking about taking *amrit*, and over Guru Arjan Dev being the first to carry a *kirpan*.
180 S. Trott (ed.), *Guidelines for the Professional Conduct of the Clergy* (London: Church House Publishing, 2015), p. 13.
181 Trott, *Guidelines for the Professional Conduct of the Clergy*.
182 M. Denscombe, *The Good Research Guide for Small Scale Social Research Projects*, fourth edition (Maidenhead: Open University Press, 2010), p. 21; R. Orsi, *Between Heaven and Earth: The Religious Worlds People Make and the Scholars who Study Them* (Princeton, NJ: Princeton University Press, 2005), p. 204.
183 T. E. Adams, S. H. Jones and C. Ellis, *Autoethnography: Understanding Qualitative Research* (Oxford: Oxford University Press, 2015), p. 17.
184 Ibid., p. 85.
185 N. Denzin, *Interpretive Autoethnography*, second edition (Los Angeles, CA and London: Sage Publishing, 2014), pp. 19–20.
186 S. Jones, T. Adams and C. Ellis (eds), "Introduction: Coming to Know Autoethnography as More than a Method", in *Handbook of Autoethnography*, first paperback edition (Walnut Creek, CA: Left Coast Press, 2015), pp. 17–47, 17, 25–6; S. Brown, "Hermeneutics in Protestant Practical Theology", in K. Cahalan and G. Mikowski (eds), *Opening the Field of Practical Theology: An Introduction* (Lanham, MD: Rowman and Littlefield, 2014), pp. 115–32, 124–5.
187 S. Pattison, *The Challenge of Practical Theology: Selected Essays*, p. 283.
188 S. Bevans, *Models of Contextual Theology*, revised and expanded edition (Maryknoll, NY: Orbis, 2002), pp. 103–16.
189 S. Pattison and J. Woodward, "An Introduction to Pastoral and Practical Theology", in J. Woodward and S. Pattison (eds), *The Blackwell Reader in Pastoral and Practical Theology* (Malden MA, and Oxford: Blackwell, 2000) pp. 1–19, here at p. 6; B. J. Miller-McLemore, "Introduction: The Contributions of Practical Theology", in B. Miller-McLemore (ed.), *The Wiley-Blackwell Companion to Practical Theology* (Malden, MA, Oxford and Chichester: Wiley-Blackwell, 2012), pp. 1–20, 14–15.
190 H. Walton, *Writing Methods in Theological Reflection* (London: SCM Press, 2014), p. 164.
191 Walton, *Writing Methods in Theological Reflection*, p. 168.

Index

3 H O *see* Sikh Dharma of the Western Hemisphere

Aart 114, 168
Abhishiktananda, Swami 12
Adams, T. E. 163, 188
Akal Taht 65 f., 68, 72, 78, 168, 170
Akhand Paath 84, 168
alcohol 23, 57, 65
Alison, J. 77, 83, 156
allegiance 44, 66, 97, 99, 108
Alpha group 41
Amar Das, Guru 31
amicism 2, 143–46, 148, 150, 168
Amir (or *emir*) 85, 168, 170 f.
Amrit 65 f., 73 f., 92, 94, 99, 109, 168, 171, 177 f., 183, 188
Amritdhari 55, 66 f., 73, 99, 149, 154, 168, 170, 178, 180, 188
Anand karaj 34, 73, 168
Angad, Guru 48, 54
Anglo-Sikh Wars 7
Anthony, A. K. 187
Apel, W. 187
apostasy 47, 49
Appiah, K. A. 15, 163
appreciative enquiry 160, 162
Ardas 26, 30, 91, 95, 168 f.
Ariarajah, W. 181
artefacts 153
atonement 33
Austin, F. 163, 179
autoethnography 3, 157 f., 160, 163, 165, 168, 190
Awagaun 43, 169

Back-and-Forth Riteing 11
Bahjan, Yog 72
Bala, Bhai 129, 138
Bani 66, 169
baptism 45 f., 80
Bardesley, W. 154
Basics of Sikhi 72
Beacon Church 1, 22–26, 76, 79, 81, 86, 100, 108, 109, 118, 136, 176, 183
beliefs 2, 14, 19, 42–45, 58, 108, 119, 157, 168, 179
betrayal 47 f., 61, 147, 166, 179
Betterment Distancing 145, 148
Bhago, Mai 78
Bhai, W., Pandit 68
Bhogal, I. 101, 184
Birmingham 3, 22, 45, 61, 87, 89, 96, 106, 151, 174
  Birmingham Council of Christian Churches 146
  HM Prison 1
BME United, Co. 154
Book of Nanak, The 125, 167, 185
Borja 125
borrowing, religious 13 f.
Bragt, M. V. 175
Brahmin 75, 131
British Sikh Report
  2013 188
  2014 178
  2017 180
Brown, S. 188
Buddha 4, 58, 114, 142, 165 f., 187
Buddhism 8, 12 f., 117, 121, 184

Cahalan, K. 163, 188
Casey, L. 174

INDEX

caste 9, 13, 31, 65, 69, 74–77, 89, 100, 104, 133, 138, 169, 182
challenges to MRP 51–65, 84
Chapman, C. 17, 164, 176
Chaur sahib 29, 93, 169
Cheetham, D. 145, 164, 187
Christ *see* Jesus, follower of
Christian identity 2, 13, 79–83, 86, 104, 112, 121, 160
Christian-Sikh 14, 102 f., 181, 184
Christmas 42, 69, 86
Chryssides, G. 164, 178, 187
Church of England 5, 14, 16, 22, 37, 47, 96, 156, 164, 169, 174
    Church of England Inter-Faith Consultative Group 175, 179
    see also Presence and Engagement
Clooney, F. X. 164, 185
Coffey, G. 183
cognitive dissonance 45, 50, 60, 107, 109, 164 f., 179
Collingwood, C. 120, 184
Cohn-Sherbok, D. 166, 176, 180 f.
Cole, O. 68, 164, 181
colonialism 18 f., 67
competition between religions 15, 146, 181
Contemplation to Attain Love 125
conversion 8, 13, 66, 69 f., 72, 154
converts 30, 40, 42, 46, 57, 59, 61, 69 f., 72 f., 98, 100, 125, 169, 181
Cooper, J. 164, 179
Cornille, C. 164, 175 f., 183

Daswandh 85, 169
Davies, C. A. 182
Dayam, J. P. 165, 175
defilement 94
Degh 169 f., 183
Denscombe, M. 188
Denzin, N. 188
Devsi, B. S. 28, 30–32, 35, 40, 54, 65 f., 76, 84, 91, 93–95, 132, 138, 141 f., 154 f., 177, 179 f., 183
Dharam Parsha Committee 164, 178
Dharma 126, 169, 181

Dhillon, B. S. 186
Dhillon, H. 164, 186
Diocesan Interfaith Adviser (DIFA) 5, 12, 35, 40, 48, 63, 75, 110 f., 119, 122, 150, 153, 156, 169, 184
discernment 60, 64, 101 f., 107, 113, 118 f., 122, 137, 143, 146 f., 150, 184
doctrine, attitude towards 4 f., 45, 80, 112, 117
dual belonging 11
Durbar 28, 32, 77, 88, 97
Dutton, M. L. 186
Dyson, D. 82, 154

Eddo-Lodge, R. 174
Ek Niwas 48, 58, 104, 169
Ellis, C. 164, 166, 189
espoused and operative theology 62, 64
ethics 42, 47, 156, 168
ethnography 77, 158, 165–67, 178 f., 180, 182 f.
evangelism 72, 86, 141, 166, 171, 175
exclusivism 15, 43

family 12, 27, 32, 45–47, 60, 73–75, 85, 91, 127, 138, 170, 175, 177, 179
Fenech, L. E. 167, 180 f., 183
fieldwork 22, 55, 62, 76, 90, 92, 104 f., 108, 152, 155f., 157
    end of 93–95
Five Ks 65, 94, 168, 170, 178
food 25, 31 f., 39, 86–88, 93, 129, 134, 171, 177, 180
Friedrich, F. 187
friendliness 87, 98, 109, 123, 136, 142–48
friendship 2, 13, 47, 49, 55, 58, 86 f., 92, 95, 123–47, 158, 163, 165, 185–87
    authority and 137, 139
    difference and 140 f.
    perfection and 140
    shadow side 137
Fuchs, K. 47
Funk, R. W. 185

Galupo, M. P. 186
Gandhi, I. 9, 114
Gaston, R. 13, 17, 165, 176, 179
Geldhof, J. 166, 175
gender 2, 23, 77–79, 83, 100, 161, 183
Geffré, C. 176
Gidoomal, R. 187
Griffiths, B. 12
Gobind Sarvar 58, 169
Gobind Singh, Guru, sons of 69
Gonzalez, K. A. 186
Gospel of Jesus According to the Jesus Seminar, the 125, 185
Gora/gori 9, 72–74, 82, 99, 102, 169
Goshen-Gotstein, A. 165, 169, 186 f.
grace 7, 28, 31, 42f., 59, 68, 81, 130, 132, 139, 170
Granthi 29–32, 35, 46, 57, 88, 94, 169
Gregg, S. E. 164, 178, 187
Guest, Keen and Nettlefold 27
guided reflection 41, 44, 57, 63, 154–56
Guru Granth Sahib Ji 1, 9, 27–32, 35 f., 38–40, 42, 44, 46, 58, 68f., 77, 81, 84, 93, 113, 115, 138, 140, 142, 167–73, 177, 182, 186–89
Gurdas, Bhai 68
Gurdwara
  attendance at 151–53
  description of 26–33
Gurmukh 158
Gurmukhi 28 f., 40, 54, 113, 158, 169, 178
Guru Ka Niwas Gurdwara (GKN) 26 f., 29, 36, 40 f., 57 f., 66 f., 69, 75, 104, 151, 179
  Committee 29, 32, 54, 76, 78, 88 f., 90, 93
  Community Association 151
  membership 76, 93, 109
  and nationalism 71
  Secretary 29–32, 41, 84, 86, 90, 94, 97
  President 31, 35, 54, 76, 93, 95
Guru Nanak, *see* Nanak, Guru Dev Ji.
Harmander Sahib 66, 68, 75, 85, 96, 168 f., 172
  attack on 68, 70 f.
Hawley, M. 183
healing 5, 30, 33, 59, 61 f., 127, 160
Hindu 5, 7 f., 9, 12 f., 48, 60, 67, 69, 75, 85, 111 f., 115–18, 126, 130, 134, 138, 141, 150, 170 f., 173, 181, 184
Holy Communion 1, 7 f., 22–26, 31, 37, 57, 63, 92 f., 139
Hooker, P. M. 165
Hukam 100, 131, 133 f., 169, 184
Hukamnama 28, 30, 34, 59, 84, 96, 167, 169
Hwyl 25, 169
hybrid religion 11
hyphenated Christianity 11, 103

identity 6, 15, 20, 46, 54, 63, 77, 79, 83, 117, 145, 150, 156, 158 *see also* Christian identity, Religious identity, *Sikhi*
idolatry 28, 47, 49, 59
Ikk Oan Kar 44, 169
imagination 123–36, 145, 150, 163
inclusivism 15, 18
India 9, 32, 68, 70 f., 84, 88, 177
injustice 19, 71, 137
interfaith 5, 10, 19–122, 174
  Interfaith Network of the United Kingdom 20, 69
  Inter Faith Wolverhampton 99, 154
interreligious prayer 15–17, 175
interspiritual age 14
Isandarova, N. 159
Izzat 73 f., 170

Jallianwala Bagh massacre 71
Janam-sakhi 102, 140, 170
Jap Ji 170, 183
Jat 67, 75, 170
Jathedar 66, 68, 170
Jenoi 67, 170
Jesudason, P. 165, 175

Jesus 68, 81, 87, 96, 101 f., 113, 117, 119–21
  arrest of 132 f.

author's vision of 4 f.
calling his disciples 129 f.
denial of 94
axorcism by 130 f.
loyalty to 100
follower of 101 f.
preaching 128
resurrection of 25, 42 f., 100, 133 f.
sketch of, *see* sketch
temptation of 126
with the children 127
Jhutti-Johal, J. 165, 182 f.
Jones, S. H. 164, 188
Juss, S. S. 186

Kaccha, Kachh or *Kachera* 65, 170
Kainth, V. 185
Kanga 65, 170
Kara 65, 67, 170
Karah Parshad 25, 31, 42, 115, 170
Karma 69 f., 118, 170
Kartarpur 102, 134
Kaur, B. J. 78
Kerney, B. L. 137, 165, 186
Kesh 65, 170
Keshdhari 67, 170
Khalistan 70, 101, 170
Khalsa 9, 34, 65–67, 70, 72, 102, 165, 168, 170–73, 178
Khanda 85, 170 f., 183
Khidrana 78
Kirat karna 85 f., 170
Kirpan 31, 65, 71, 170, 178, 188
Kirtan 29, 170
Knitter, P. F. 165, 176
Kshatriyas 75
Küng, H. 80 f., 165, 183

Lalo 131
Lamb, C. 17, 165, 176
Lambert, R. 68, 181
Langar 30–32, 34 f., 55, 74, 102, 134, 170 f.
language 39 f., 49, 52, 54, 109, 113 f. 158, 169, 178
Lee, K.-W. 186

liturgy 81, 113, 172, 184
lived religion 14, 108–10, 119, 122
Loehlin, C. H. 68
Lohar 75, 170

McCabe, J. 187
McLaren, B. 142, 146, 166, 187
McLeod, H. 67, 166, 180
Meilaender, G. C. 185
Mandla *v* Dowell Lee 72
Mann Jitt Weekly 69, 99
Manmukh 42, 91, 95, 158, 170
Mardana 69, 39, 131, 138
Margalit, A. 46, 49, 61, 167, 180
meditation 9, 44, 85 f., 96, 98, 104, 115, 144, 151, 170, 172, 181, 183
Mehat, N. 178
Midland Langar Seva Society 87 f.
Mikowski, G. 188
Miller, S. K. 12, 48, 166, 175, 179
Miller-McLemore, B. J. 163, 166, 188 f.
Miri piri 85, 170 f.
Misl 75 f., 171f.
missionaries 12, 67 f., 100, 120
Mona 67, 171
Monchanin, J. 12
Mool Mantra or *Mul Mantra* 28, 42, 138, 168, 171
money 28, 30, 32, 36, 38, 66, 85 f., 95, 129, 177, 179
Moyaert, M. 166, 175
Muhammad 4, 142
Mukti 43, 142, 171
Multi-self 145
Multiple Religious Belonging (MRB) 11, 18, 21, 77, 171
Multiple Religious Participation (MRP)
 asymetry in 154
 choice of term 11
 significance of 11–21
 suppression of 106 f.
Multiple Religious Practice 11
Mulvey, L. 183
Muslim 5, 7, 9, 12, 16, 27, 48, 65, 69 f., 81, 88, 109, 112, 121, 130, 138, 141, 150, 159, 171 f., 184

mysticism 80, 151

Naam Karan 31, 171
Naaman 61, 180
Nanak, Guru Dev Ji 8, 27, 48 f., 65, 70, 77, 87, 100, 102, 109, 112, 121, 130, 138, 141, 150, 159, 171 f., 184
    feeding the Sadhus 128
    in Kartarpur 134
    and Lalo 131
    listlessness as a youth 127 f.
    and the Pirs 131 f., 141
    "There is no Hindu, there is no Muslim" 48, 69, 130, 150
Nanak Shah Fakir 125
narrative in research 150, 158, 160
    narrative tension 108
    narrative verdict 108
    problems with 160 f.
Nirgun sargun 45, 171
Nirvair 139, 171
Nishan sahib 27, 171

O'Brien, K. 185
Oberoi, H. 67, 166, 180
observer 39, 87, 112, 152
Orientalism 20, 65, 171, 176
Orsi, R. 188

Pangat 69, 171
Panikkar, R. 81, 183
Panj pyare 70, 72, 74, 171
Parchar 72, 171
Parry, J. 68, 87, 166, 178, 181
particularism 15
passing over 13
Patit 66, 171
pattern of life 55–59
Pattison, S. 155, 163, 166, 180, 184, 188
permission to research 51–55, 63, 153, 156 f.
Permission to Smile 146
Phan, P. 18 f., 166
Philia 137, 171
Pieris, A. 12, 176
Pir 85, 131 f., 141, 170 f.

playfulness 13, 56, 63, 123, 145
pluralism 15, 18, 117
post-colonial 18, 181
practical theology 3, 19, 121, 150, 159–61, 163, 165 f., 180, 184, 188 f.
Prasad 35, 171
prayer 15–17, 24, 30, 61 f., 84, 93, 96, 110, 113, 117, 120, 166, 168, 175
    at dawn 66
    at home 84 f.
preferences, religious 108
Premawardhana, D. 176
Presence and Engagement 5, 99, 166, 171, 175
Puja 114, 171
Punjab 68, 70 f., 82, 170
Punjabiat 82, 171, 172
Purohit, K. 181

racism 9, 11, 74, 174, 181
Rajput, A. 159
Rajkumar, P. J. R. 165, 175
Ramadan 17, 110
Ramgarhia 27, 75 f., 89, 91, 172
    Ramgarhia Association 71, 84
Rand, K. 45, 178
Ravidass, Guru 172, 182
Ravidassi 48, 74 f., 104, 172, 182
Redding, A. H. 109, 121, 185
Rehat Maryada 65 f., 94, 99, 172
reflection 26, 62 f., 63, 78, 85, 153
    reflection-in-action 110, 118
    reflection-on-action 110, 118
    reflection partner 41, 44, 57
    reflective practice 155, 167, 189
reincarnation 42 f., 117, 142, 169
relationalism 15, 144
religiosity 42, 49, 141
religious experience 4 f., 7, 15, 49, 58
religious identity 7, 11, 15 f., 18–20, 46, 48, 57, 106, 114 f., 121, 142, 146, 150, 154, 178
    Christian religious identity 79–82, 112, 160, 164 166, 183, 187
    hyphenated identity 102 f.

Sikh religious identity 65–70, 166 f., 174, 180, 182
research
  academic adviser 41, 56, 155 f.
  accountability 155 f.
  computer analysis 155 f.
  insights from 136, 149 f.
  interviews 12, 34, 40, 43, 59, 61, 72 f., 87, 101, 105, 109, 112, 115, 118, 154–57, 177, 179, 183 f.
  journal 26, 47, 153, 155 f.
  method 136, 152–56, 159
  permission for 51–55, 153, 156 f.
  principles 156–60
  risk of harm 149, 157, 161 *see also* ethics, focus groups, guided reflection
resurrection 25, 42 f., 100, 125, 133 f., 176
Rodrigo, M. 12
Ryan, T. 175

Sach khand 35 f., 172
Sahajdhari 66 f., 149, 172
Sai Baba Mandir 185
Said, A. 176
Saini, P. S. 71
Salaat 114, 172
Sambhi, P. S. 68, 164, 181
Sangat 49, 78, 83 f., 95, 102, 142, 172
Sanghera, J. 182
Sanghera, S. 178, 182
Sant 132, 172, 185
Sant Nirankari 48, 172
Sarna, S. 167, 185
Sato, K. 75, 182
Say "No" to Violence Against Women and Girls 78
Schön, D. 109, 118
Scripture 23, 43, 137, 141 f., 173 *see also Guru Granth Sahib Ji*
Scriptural Reasoning 15, 68, 181
sectarianism 71, 138, 181
secularism 4, 20, 49, 65, 70, 73, 118, 143, 186
self-questionnaire 102–5, 107, 155 f.

sexuality 77, 79 f., 83, 161
shadow side 4, 33, 137, 140, 147
Sherwood, H. 181, 184
Shiromani Gurdwara Parbandhak Committee 66, 172
Shahada 121, 172
Shinto 12
Shri Venkateswara (Balaji) Temple, Tividale 5, 7 f., 174
Shudras 75
Shukriya 31, 172
Sian, K. P. 181
Sikh Dharma of the Western Hemisphere, the 72
Sikh Federation UK 72
Sikh-Christian 101–3, 107, 149, 184
Sikh-Christian Forum 68
Sikhi
  choice of for MRP 8, 152
  ethnicity 20, 72–74
  religion 42 f., 65–70, 84–86
  nationality 70 f.
  practical outworkings 85–87
  and secularism 70
  use of term 174
Sikhism, *see Sikhi.*
Simran 30, 85, 136, 142, 151, 172, 179, 183
Singh, B. V. 68
Singh, G. 68, 177, 186
Singh, H. 181
Singh, P. 69, 180 f., 183
Singh, Princess S. T. 78
Singh, T. 68
Singh Sabha 68, 172
Siropa 94, 153, 172
sketch 123–25
slavery 181
Smith, A. 17, 167, 176
social factors 109
Srebrenica Day 6, 9, 174
status 73, 147 f.
  author's status 27, 39
stereotyping 79
street missions, see *parchar.*
Stobert, M. 41, 44, 142, 154

Strange, D. 59 f., 167, 180
Stringer, M. 43, 62, 167, 178–80
study of religions 13 f., 108–10, 164, 178 f., 182
submission 39, 61, 81, 108–10, 164, 178 f., 182
subversive fulfilment 59
Sudworth, R. 17, 176
Suffragette 78
Sufi 112, 115, 131
Sukhmani Sahib 93 f., 172
Sundays 27, 37, 55, 95
Superdiversity 14, 172
syncretism 11, 16, 80

Takhat 29, 31, 34, 94, 173
Takhar, O. K. 66, 75, 167, 180, 182
Takht 173 *see also Akal Taht*
Tankah 66, 173
Tarkhan 75, 132, 173
Tenth Gate mysticism 151
theodicy 140, 173
thick relationship 47 f., 98
Thompson, K. G. 109
Thompson, V. A. 187
transcendentalism 44 f.
Trinity 45, 80, 87
Trott, S. 188
Trumpp, E. 68
Tu, J. I. 185
Tuckett, C. M. 187
turban 29, 56, 63, 66, 71, 107
  picture of author with 56 f., 107

universalism 16, 44 f., 50, 69, 158, 169

Vaisakhi 34 f., 100 f., 174
Vaishyas 75
Valmiki 75
vegetarianism 55, 88, 180, 188
Vedic religions 8, 42, 69, 80

Vento, J. M. 187
violence 6, 36, 70, 73, 78, 101
Volf, M. 6, 174
volunteers 32, 88, 110
Voss Roberts, M. 77, 176, 183
Vukalić, S. 174

Waand chhakna (or *vand ke chakna*) 85, 174
Waheguru 30, 35, 46, 85, 104, 172 f., 180
Waheguru ji ka Kalsa, Waheguru ji ki fate 41, 173
Walton, H. 163, 167, 189
Wardell, M. 178, 187
Ways of Meeting and the Theology of Religions 145, 164, 187
wedding 27 f., 33 f., 73, 177
white 22, 29 f., 54, 71 f., 73 f., 77 f., 106, 111, 184 *see also gora*
Wingate, A. 17, 167, 176
worship 7 f., 11, 18, 36, 39 f., 81, 116 f., 151
  Christian 1, 22–26, 46, 95 f., 177
  images 28, 114 f.
  non-Christian 16 f., 47, 60, 111 f. 111–21, 152, 157, 184
  Sikh 1, 26–31, 57, 69, 73
World Community for Christian Meditation 85, 170, 179
World Council of Churches 15 f., 110, 165, 175, 181

Yagnopavitam 126, 141, 173
Yeshu Satsang 181

Zat 75, 126, 141, 173
Zen 120, 184

EU GPSR Authorized Representative:

LOGOS EUROPE, 9 rue Nicolas Poussin, 17000 La Rochelle, France

contact@logoseurope.eu

www.ingramcontent.com/pod-product-compliance
Lightning Source LLC
Chambersburg PA
CBHW060953230426
43665CB00015B/2180